Study Gu

the worry free *Life*

TAKE CONTROL OF YOUR THOUGHT LIFE BY
weeding out the bad and nurturing the good!

*CLINICALLY PROVEN AND FAITH-BASED

TERENCE J. SANDBEK, PH.D.
PATRICK W. PHILBRICK

THE WORRY FREE LIFE: *Study Guide*

Terence J. Sandbek Ph.D. & Patrick W. Philbrick

Copyright © 2008 Green Valley Publishing L.L.C.

Green Valley Publishing LLC
4300 Auburn Blvd., Suite 206
Sacramento, Ca 95841
(530) 621-3098

Find us on the Web at: www.TheWorryFreeLife.com
Books may be ordered from: Orders@TheWorryFreeLife.com
Readers may contact the authors by email: Support@TheWorryFreeLife.com

Chief Editor: Letha Scanzoni
Cover Design and Layout: Libby Nicholson, gocreativeonline.com

Unattributed quotations are by Terence J. Sandbek and Patrick W. Philbrick

ISBN, printed. 978-1-59971-929-0

Printed and bound in the United States of America

The Worry Free Life
Study Guide Outline

Do not conform any longer to the pattern of this world, but be transformed by the renewing of your mind. Then you will be able to test and approve what God's will is-his good, pleasing and perfect will.
— *Romans 12:2*

Purpose

The purpose of this course is not insight but rather teaching you mental, emotional and behavioral strategies for making your life better. Consequently, it is not enough to merely think about what you learn, nor even feel good about it. You need to practice your new skills on a daily and weekly basis.

Small Group Guidelines

What we are not:

We are not a therapy group.
We are not victims of our past.
We are not here to solve other people's problems.
We are not dependent for change based on the skill of the facilitator.
We are not anti-science (psychology).
We are not looking for a magic bullet.

What we are:

We are contributors as well as receivers in this group.
We are committed to significant short-term change.
We are a group of equals, no one is more important than any other.
We are a group of people learning how to live a God-filled life.
We are more interested in the how than the why.
We focus on the present.
We are devoted to learning new life skills.
We are people who believe that psychology can enhance theology.
We are active participants in achieving our dreams.
We are dedicated to taking personal responsibility for our own lives.

Today is the tomorrow I worried about yesterday.

Guidelines for Discussion Leaders

1. **Use the Study Guide with the book**. Have each study group member read the corresponding chapter in *The Worry Free Life* prior to discussing it in the group.

2. **The first meeting**. Make sure everyone in the group has *The Worry Free Life* and the companion Study Guide. After the opening prayer, have everyone introduce themselves and use an icebreaker such as "What is my favorite junk food." Read the Small Group Guidelines in whichever way is most comfortable for the group: one person can read them; each person can read one; etc.

3. **Prepare for each meeting ahead of time**. You will need a working knowledge of each chapter from the book and from the study guide. You will want to do all the exercises for yourself so that you can better understand how they will be used.

4. **Be flexible**. Although the study guide was designed for doing one chapter each meeting, you can go at a more leisurely pace if necessary.

5. **Encourage people to be involved**. Someone can volunteer to bring snacks (a different person each week), others may get the room prepared, some can be greeters. Get others to help you do whatever can be done to make the group run better and relieve you of the details.

6. **Know your role**. Make it clear that you are merely the facilitator and may not have any special knowledge that other group members lack. You may spend a lot of time in the group saying, "I don't know." Each member can and will learn from the others.

7. **Begin and end on time**. Although this may seem trivial, it is part of the learning process. Don't wait for everyone to arrive before starting.

8. **How long to meet?** Pat and Terry do this course in ten weeks of 2-hour sessions. As a group, decide how long you would like it to last. Many of the members we have taught want more so we are considering designing a graduate course.

9. **Consider child care**. You may want to arrange for someone to meet with the children in a room away from the location of your course.

10. **We are here to help**. Please remember that any questions you have can be answered by emailing us at *support@TheWorryFreeLife.com*

The Worry Free Life
Session #1: Your Garden

Do not conform any longer to the pattern of this world, but be transformed by the renewing of your mind. Then you will be able to test and approve what God's will is-his good, pleasing and perfect will.
— Romans 12:2

The Garden Metaphor

Romans 12:2, "The patterns of this world," refers to the thoughts, beliefs, and interpretations common in our culture. Renewing your mind, simply put means thought catching the silent assumptions and automatic thinking that exist on the barely perceptible edges of our awareness that have a profound effect on how we feel and behave.

After catching these thoughts we can examine them for validity. Then replace them with the truth; more accurate statements that are healthy and get us moving forward. The garden is our metaphor for the things in life that God gives you stewardship over and responsibility for.

Writing

Writing is essential to the Worry Free Life because so many thoughts, beliefs, and interpretations exist on the outer edge of our awareness. We cannot capture, remember, or examine them for validity unless we get in the habit of writing them down.

Property Lines

The Property Line around your garden symbolizes the limit of what you can control. You can act to influence other people and life events but you can never control them. Your Property Line is basically your skin. You are responsible for and control only things inside of yourself. Nothing you can do can control what another person thinks or feels. The things you can potentially control are your thoughts, emotions, sensations, and behaviors.

Goal:

One thing I would like to get out of this book.

1

Property Lines

Another homework assignment will be to learn how to define your property lines. You want to become clear as to what is inside and what is outside your property lines. This can be hard because other people can confuse you by telling you where your property lines are. God has made you the steward of our life and only you can determine what your property lines are.

Complete this Property Line Questionnaire.

Define which one of the following situations is within your property line and which ones are not. Remember, only those things that are within your control are within your property line.

	Situation	In	Out
1	Your mother is mad at you because she thinks you ruined her Thanksgiving by not coming for dinner; instead you had dinner with your friends		
2	You are angry because the car in front of you just cut you off.		
3	Your wife/husband calls you stupid because you forgot to pick up one of the things on the shopping list when you went to the store.		
4	You know people at work who you insist do not deserve a promotion. This situation gets you to hate your job and only perform at 50% when you are there		
5	For years you have been mad at your parents because you think they favor your sibling more than you.		
6	Your teenage son is hurt and upset at you because you decided you could not afford to buy him the new motorcycle you promised him.		
7	You overhear your coworkers talking about how selfish they think you are because you accepted the promotion for a job that they themselves wanted. You clearly knew they wanted the job, and they have been with the company longer than you.		
8	Your husband/wife/child makes you feel so angry when they forget to do things you asked them to do.		
9	"Life Sucks!!!!!!! Nothing good ever happens to me. I'll never feel like I did in the good old days."		
10	You are a husband and your wife says, "We've got to talk." You instantly panic.		
11	You are a wife and when you try to tell your husband you feel hurt about something he said, he replies, "I don't want to discuss it" and walks out the room. He refuses to talk to you for four days.		

This is how we see property line issues in the situations above:

1. You cannot control your mother's anger-only your response to it.
2. You cannot control the behavior of the other driver, but you can decide whether you want to feel angry.
3. You cannot make your spouse stop calling you names; you can speak up about how you feel about it.
4. Of course good things happen to people who do not deserve them. However, it really has nothing to do with whether you like or dislike your job. It is still the same job.
5. It is unfortunate that your parents may have favored your sibling. You can't change it, so find a way to adapt.

2

6. Your teenage son has a right to be upset even if it is for the wrong reasons. You can choose how you want to deal with it.
7. No one has the power to stop the wagging of tongues. How you handle it is within your property line.
8. You need to decide whether anger is something you want to feel or if it is a motivator for getting them to change. You do not have to be angry. Or you can choose to do so. It is up to you.
9. Life goes on for good or bad. Your only choice is what you are going to do about it.
10. Get used to it, men. Women need to talk. Learning to listen and be a part of their verbal world is much better for you than avoidance and panic.
11. You cannot control your husband's behavior. If it is important you tell someone about how you feel, you will need to find alternatives: a close friend, a relative, a professional counselor.

Begin a Success Journal

Reason for doing this
For many people, the end of the day means falling asleep think of all the day's failures. You need to learn how to end each day concentrating on what you did right. You want to switch from seeing the day as half full rather than half empty.

You need to be able to identify and name your successes. If you are more familiar noticing your failures, you may miss seeing many successes. As you become more successful in your journey, you may miss seeing some of your successes because they may look unfamiliar to you. Successes that have impact are those that are identified and named.

How to do it
Make this the last think you do at night. Be especially watchful for very small successes — a brick house is not made out of one big brick but rather many thousands of small, insignificant bricks. Be especially watchful for your successes with your homework assignments — identify what you do rather than what you failed to do. A success is something you do, not something that happened to you — winning the lottery is not a success.

Benefits for doing it
You will immediately begin to have a more positive perspective on your achievements. Down the road you will be able to look back and find out how far you have traveled. During a setback you will find out that you do not have to start over because you have gone farther than you expected

How to Sabotage Your Program for Self Improvement

If you want to ensure that this course will not work for you, follow these steps . . . . .

1. Don't do any of the assignments.
2. If you must do them, do them only half-heatedly; try not to concentrate too much while you are working on them.
3. While you are working on one problem, try to think of all the other problems you have.
4. Deny any improvement, especially when it's small.
5. Refuse to believe that these new skills will work for you.
6. In case you fail at #6, think that these things do not apply to your situation because you are different.
7. Be sure to continue to tell yourself you are beyond help.
8. Drop out of this course and look for a magic solution somewhere else.
9. Try to spend as much of your time as possible engaging in negative thinking.
10. Be sure to take responsibility only for failure but not for success.

How do you sabotage your life's journey?

Grace Partner

Find a Grace Partner that you can share this course with on a regular basis. You may use the sample form below for keeping track of your shared time with your Grace Partner.

Grace Partner
Weekly Follow Up

Name of your grace partner _____

Partner's phone # _____

Write down any of successes you and your partner achieved this week:

1.

2.

3.

4.

5.

What goal are you both trying to achieve by the worry free life?

Have both of you been able to find the time to do their writing assignments?

Each of you name one healthy and one unhealthy emotion you have seen in your own life.

Prayer requests

Discussion Questions

1   How would I describe my property line? Is it well-defined? Built of sturdy material? Changeable?

2   Do I ever let others change my property line for me? If so who and under what circumstances?

3   Once I get the proper tools, how would I like to make my property line like I want it?

4   How will my life be different once my property is more clearly marked and my garden cared for?

5   What might God think about me improving my property line?

For more information on information your property lines, see chapter 1 in *The Worry Free Life.*

The Worry Free Life
Session #2: The Big H

I've learned by now to be quite content whatever my circumstances. I'm just as happy with little as with much, with much as with little. I've found the recipe for being happy whether full or hungry, hands full or hands empty. Whatever I have, wherever I am, I can make it through anything in the One who makes me who I am.
—Philippians 4:11-12, MSG

Writing

Writing is the only way we can slow our minds down enough to capture the silent assumptions.

"Clarity is the anecdote to anxiety" Marcus Buckingham.

The promises of more happiness, less suffering, and more self-control are dependent on how well we do the homework.

Two Types of Happiness

Little "h" is dependent on and comes from things outside of us. Things like chocolate, amusement parks, good food, romance, music, and wine. Other words for the little "h" are pleasure, excitement, lust, fun, instant gratification, amusement, and entertainment.

Big "H" comes from things inside of us: Healthy thoughts, beliefs and interpretations. Feelings that come from the Big "H" are agape love, faith, contentment, satisfaction, hope, perseverance, courage, trust, peace of mind, gratitude, harmony, and flow.

Comparison of the little h and the Big H

Little h *The happiness that comes from* *the absence of pain and discomfort*	**Big H** *The happiness that comes from* *coping with pain and discomfort*
Cannot co-exist with pain	Can co-exist with pain
Comes from outside of you: Life	Comes from within you: Self
Is easy to get because there are so many places to find it	Is difficult to get because there are only 4 places to find it
Only lasts a short while	Can last forever
You have no control over whether you get it or not	Potentially, you have control over whether you get it

B*E*S*T

The only things I can control in life and am responsible for are the things God has given me stewardship over are my:

Behavior   **Emotions**   **Sensations/Stress**   **Thoughts**

Happiness is not a goal in life but rather a by-product of something else. That something else is self control. Rather than letting your life run you, you need to learn the skills to control your life so that you can experience it the way God intended you to. By controlling behavior, emotions, sensations/stress, and thoughts you can find your pathway to the Big H. Out of the four, thoughts, is your most important resource.

Dominoes

The order of the "Dominoes" is always:

Life
    Thoughts
        Feelings
            Behavior
                Consequences

Complete the Dominoes Questionnaire on the next page

1. Identify a situation—past or present—that is or was difficult for you.
2. Discover what was happening for each of the dominoes.
3. Remember that the first domino (Life) and last domino (Consequence) refer to events outside you.
4. Do one questionnaire each day for a week picking a different situation each day.

Life Domino

- ☐ Were you at work or home?
- ☐ Were there other people present?
- ☐ Were you doing anything unusual?
- ☐ Was anyone making the situation difficult for you?
- ☐ Other:

Thought Domino

- ☐ Were you putting yourself down?
- ☐ Were you using labels about yourself?
- ☐ Was your thinking muddled?
- ☐ Was your mind racing?
- ☐ Other:

Feeling Domino-Emotion

Were you depressed?
Were you feeling guilty?
Were you feeling helpless?
Were you resentful?
Were you anxious?
Were you fearful?
Other:

Feeling Domino - Sensations

- ☐ Were you feeling nauseous?
- ☐ Did you have butterflies?
- ☐ Did you have a headache?
- ☐ Were you tired or fatigued?
- ☐ Did you have a panic attack?
- ☐ Did you hyperventilate?
- ☐ Were your muscles tense?
- ☐ Other:

Behavior Domino

- ☐ Did you shut down and do nothing?
- ☐ Did you punish yourself?
- ☐ Did you run away?
- ☐ Did you retaliate?
- ☐ Did you avoid something?
- ☐ Did you insulate yourself from others?
- ☐ Other:

Consequence Domino

- ☐ Did you end up in the hospital?
- ☐ Were you abandoned?
- ☐ Did anyone try to hurt you?
- ☐ Did you lose anything, i.e., your job?
- ☐ Other:

Worry Vs. Concern

Worry is unhealthy and comes from thinking that we can control things outside of us. Concern is healthy thinking about things inside of us that are potentially within our control.

Worry	Concern
Thinking we can control people and things outside of our property line.	Healthy thinking that accepts our limitations about life

Similarities	Differences
Both can take up a lot of time and effort - intensive	Worry: concentrates on the unchangeable Concern: focus on what we can change
Both deal with important issues	Worry: cyclic in nature - no forward movement Concern: is linear
Both are a mental process	Worry: Absolute waste of time Concern: Necessary

Give several examples of how you get trapped into the Worry cycle.

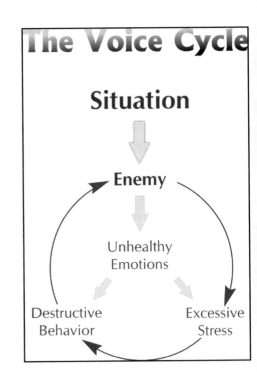

How will your life be different when you have broken this vicious cycle?

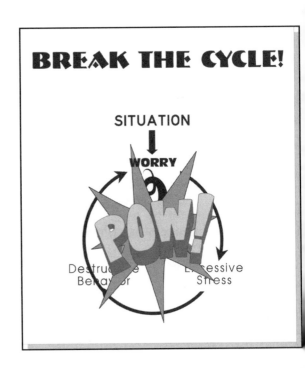

Discussion Questions

1. Make a list of little "h" activities you have experienced recently that have brought you pleasure.

2. Think of someone you admire who has the Big "H." How might their life be different than yours?

3. What did you learn by completing the Domino Questionnaire?

4. How you would explain the difference between worry and concern to another person?

5. Read Philippians 4:11 and describe what Paul might have been thinking and feeling when he wrote this passage.

For more information on the Big H, Dominoes, and the Worry Cycle, see chapter 2 in *The Worry Free Life.*

The Worry Free Life
Session #3: Emotions

Why do you let your emotions take over, lashing out and spitting fire? — Job 15:12

Feelings

Feelings can be either sensations or emotions.

Sensations

Sensations are feelings that come from the physical body. Some examples are: mucle fatigue, hunger, thirst, physical pain, sexual urges, drug & alcohol cravings, etc.

Partial List of Sensations

Ache	Desire	Numb	Sluggish
Arousal	Dull	Panicky	Tense
Blah	Fidgety	Passion	Thirsty
Brisk	Flat	Relaxed	Tightness
Calm	Hunger	Restful	Tired
Composed	Infatuation	Sexy	Uptight
Craving	Lust	Shaky	Yearn

Stress

We generally confuse stress with two other things: things that happen to you and what you experience as the result of stress. The things that happen to you that get you stressed are called triggers or stressors. Examples of things that you experience as the result of stress are: fatigue, lack of concentration, insomnia, memory loss, and appetite increase or decrease. Stress is a brain function designed to keep us alive. Our brain contains something called the Central Nervous System [CNS]. This is the same for all animals.

There are two parts to the CNS: the Sympathetic Nervous System (which we will call the Activation Response) and the Parasympathetic Nervous System (which we will call the Relaxation Response). They act like the opposite ends of a seesaw. You can only turn one on by turning the other one off. They can't both be on or off at the same time.

The Activation Response is turned on when our brain aware of real or imagined danger. The Activation Response automatically turns on some body functions: rapid breathing, muscle tension, racing mind. It simultaneously turns other functions off: the digestive system, the reproductive system, and the immune system. When the danger goes away, everything is reversed. The Relaxation Response gets turned on and Activation Response is turned off. Everything turned on (rapid breathing, etc.) gets turned off. Everything turned off (immune system, etc.) gets turned on. Humans have one additional method for turning on the Activation Response (getting stressed) that other animals don't have. This method is the most common trigger for setting off stress. It is called worry.

Managing stress involves 2 skills: turning on the Relaxation Response and eliminating the most common trigger, worry. Turning on the Relaxation Response involves 3 skills: Natural Breathing, Muscle Relaxation, Mind Calming (different from changing thoughts).

Emotions

The reason you want to be able to tell the difference between sensations and emotions is that you will be learning separate skills for each. Your skills for managing your emotions will be different from those discussed in the previous paragraph.

Differences Between Sensations and Emotions

Sensations	Emotions
"Feelings" that are physical in nature	*"Feelings" that are an experience of affect that may be pleasant or unpleasant*
Rapid, improper breathing Muscle tension Racing mind Muscle pain Body fatigue Sexual urges Hunger Thirst Sleepy Cravings	Remorse, Shame Guilt Anger Resentment Rational/Irrational fear Depression Helplessness Sadness Healthy/Unhealthy anxiety

Make a list of sensation you find difficult to deal with.

Emotions Are Like Fire

Never trust your emotions when making decisions. Emotions are like fire. When controlled they can be very useful and constructive, but when allowed to rage out of control, they can be very destructive.

There are two types of emotions: healthy and unhealthy. They are also called constructive and destructive. Both types of emotions can be painful and intense.

Healthy emotions can be very painful, such as intense grief over losing a loved one or the anxiety you feel before meeting someone for the first time. Healthy emotions keep us moving and growing. Unhealthy emotions keep us stuck.

Absorbed	Cross	Fearless	Invalidated	Relief
Adoration	Crushed	Feisty	Irate	Remorse
Affectionate	Culpable	Ferocious	Irritated	Resistive
Afflicted	Daring	Festive	Isolated	Sad
Afraid	Defeated	Fondness	Jealous	Satisfied
Aggravated	Dejected	Frightened	Jolly	Scared
Aggressive	Delight	Frustrated	Jovial	Scornful
Agitated	Dependent	Fuming	Joy	Sentimental
Alarmed	Desirable	Furious	Joyous	Serene
Alienated	Determined	Generous	Jubilant	Shame
Alive	Disappointed	Glad	Jumpy	Shocked
Amused	Discontented	Gleeful	Keen	Sincere
Angry	Discouraged	Gloomy	Kindness	Somber
Anguished	Disgusted	Glum	Lighthearted	Sorrowful
Annoyed	Dislike	Grateful	Liking	Spirited
Anxiety (healthy)	Dismal	Grouchy	Lonely	Stagnant
Appalled	Dismayed	Grumpy	Loving	Stretched
Appealing	Distant	Happy	Low	Strong
Apprehensive	Distraught	Heartbroken	Loyal	Stubborn
Ardent	Distressed	Heavy-hearted	Melancholy	Suffering
Ashamed	Doubtful	Heroic	Merry	Sulky
Attraction	Dreadful	Hesitant	Moody	Sullen
Avid	Dreary	Hopeful	Mortified	Surprised
Awed	Eager	Horrified	Mournful	Sympathetic
Awkward	Earnest	Hostile	Neglected	Sympathy
Belligerent	Ecstatic	Humble	Nervous	Tearful
Bliss	Edgy	Humiliated	Offended	Tender
Boiling	Elated	Hurt	Optimistic	Threatened
Bold	Elation	Hysterical	Out of Sorts	Thrilled
Bored	Empty	Ill at Ease	Outraged	Timid
Brave	Enchantment	Immobilized	Overwhelmed	Torn
Carefree	Encouraged	Impatient	Pained	Tortured
Caring	Engrossed	Impulsive In	Peaceful	Tragic
Cautious	Enjoyment	the Dumps	Phony	Trapped
Charmed	Enraged	Incoherent	Playful	Triumphant
Cheerful	Enthralled	Independent	Pleased	Two-faced Uneasy
Cheery	Enthused	Indignant	Pleasure	Unhappy
Comfortable	Enthusiastic	Inflamed	Powerless	Upset
Compassionate	Envious	Infuriated	Pressured	Violated
Complacent	Envy	Injured	Pride	Weak
Concerned	Euphoric	Inquisitive	Proud	Weary
Confident	Evasive	Insecure	Provoked	Wrathful
Contented	Exasperated	Inspired	Quiet	Zealous
Contrite	Excited	Insulted	Rapture	Zestful
Courageous	Exhilarated	Intent	Reassured	
Cowardly	Fascinated	Interested	Regret	
Creative	Fear (rational)	Intrigued	Rejected	

List (Partial) of Healthy Emotions

Choose 5 healthy emotions from this list and use the next four steps (Coping with Healthy Emotions) to learn how to manage healthy emotional pain. Use a separate sheet of paper for your Coping Plan. Keep them in your 3-ring binder.

Coping with Healthy Emotions

Even though these healthy emotions can be quite painful, you can learn to cope with them by using the following steps.

Step #1: Observe

Notice the painful emotion (your instinct is to ignore it), but don't judge it. It is almost reflexive for humans to make a value judgment about emotional pain. For example, "Oh, this is awful," "I can't stand this." In a sense, you want to stand apart from yourself and just notice what is happening. "I'm feeling an intense sadness right now" or "I'm feeling anxiety and stress about my meeting with the boss tomorrow." When you find yourself being drawn back into the pain (evaluating, interpreting, or reacting), back away and continue to observe it.

Step #2: Define

Try to determine whether this emotional pain is healthy or unhealthy. If it is not one of the unhealthy emotions then, by default, it must be healthy. If the emotional pain is unhealthy then you need to immediately switch to your coping strategies for handling this type of emotions (you will learn this in session 7). For now, just determine if the emotion is healthy or unhealthy). If it is healthy, then try to correctly name it: sadness, anger, boredom, remorse, loneliness, anxiety, rational fear, etc.

Step #3: Accept

This important step keeps you from equating yourself with your feelings. Emotions are something you experience, not who you are. Feelings are not facts. Just because you are angry doesn't mean you are an angry person. You are always more than your emotions. By not making your emotions a standard to determine who you are, you are free to be more than your emotions, and the person God intends you to be.

Step #4: Embrace

Healthy, painful emotions exist to motivate you to better yourself. They are "God's megaphone to a deaf world." Your anger wants you to confront the situation which violates your dignity so that you can value what God has created. By crying when you are sad, you heal wounds that can keep you from reaching your divine potential. When you forgive yourself for making mistakes, you grow that much closer to the goals that God wants for you.

Destructive Emotions

As you can see there are many healthy, painful emotions. Fortunately, there are only six destructive emotions we need to be on alert for. All the hundreds of other emotions are healthy and God-honoring by default. The following table shows you healthy alternative for each destructive emotion.

Destructive vs. Constructive Emotions

Destructive	Constructive
Guilt	Remorse
Resentment	Anger
Irrational Fear	Rational Fear
Helplessness	Weakness
Depression	Sadness

Unhealthy Anxiety	Healthy Anxiety

Although these two different types of emotions may seem the same, they are radically different. The differences between these two types of painful emotions are shown in the following table.

Destructive, Painful Emotions	**Constructive, Painful Emotions**
Come from the Voice	Come from us
Long duration	Short duration
Inhibits personal and spiritual growth	Enhances personal and spiritual growth
Prompt us to engage in destructive behavior	Prompt us to engage in constructive behavior

You can remember the six destructive emotions by memorizing the phrase: **God Reigns In His Delightful Universe**. The first letter in each word stands for one of the unhealthy emotions.

Guilt
Resentment
Irrational Fear
Helplessness
Depression
Unhealthy Anxiety

Guilt
Behavior: Guilt is the emotion a person feels when he or she is punishing oneself.
Thought: Guilt is caused by the belief that he or she has violated an externally imposed rule through the use of "should" language.

Resentment
Behavior: Resentment is the emotion a person feels when he or she wants to get revenge or retaliate against other people.
Thought: Resentment is caused by the belief that because someone has violated your rights, they are bad and worthless.

Irrational Fear
Behavior: Irrational fear is the emotion a person feels when he or she is spending time insulating oneself from the real world.
Thought: Irrational fear is caused by a belief that something inside oneself (emotion, sensation) is dangerous and unsafe.

Helplessness
Behavior: Helplessness is the emotion a person feels when he or she is desperately trying to escape from a situation, i.e. running away.
Thought: Helplessness is caused by the belief that something is happening which is literally intolerable — ("I can't stand it.")

Depression
Behavior: Depression is the emotion a person feels when he or she is being lifeless. Lifelessness is not restricted to inactivity. Partying all night, gambling away a weekend, running up a credit card on a shopping binge are all considered lifeless because there is no purpose to these behaviors other than proving how worthless one is.
Thought: Depression is caused by the belief that a person has no redeeming value as a human being and is worthless.

Unhealthy Anxiety

Behavior: Unhealthy Anxiety is the emotion a person feels when he or she expends effort to avoid something that is perceived as terrible but is often blown out of proportion.

Thought: Unhealthy Anxiety is caused by the two-pronged belief that (1) something awful has a high probability of happening in the near future and (2) when it does, it will be a personally tragedy.

Discussion Questions

1. Name some of the common sensations and emotions you experience. Use the table in this session entitled "Differences Between Sensations and Emotions."

2. For those emotions you identified, which are constructive and which are destructive. Consult the table called Destructive vs. Constructive Emotions.

3. Everyone experiences the destructive emotions differently. Some people experience guilt and depression more than the others. Some may experience anxiety and fear most often. Which destructive emotions are the most common in your life?

4. Read Genesis 25:27-34. Which destructive and constructive emotions might Jacob and Esau have been feeling There is no correct answer. Use what you have learned in this session to make an educated guess.

5. Think of a time in your life when you experienced healthy, painful emotions. If you were experiencing these today how could you use the above four steps to manage the emotions in a healthy way. The four steps are: Observe, Define, Accept, Embrace.

For more information on emotions, see chapter 3 in *The Worry Free Life*.

The Worry Free Life Session #4:
The Pests Get In the Garden

And then he added, "It is the thought-life that defiles you."
— Mark 7:20

The Voice

A powerful technique for managing your worry is to put it outside of you and give ownership to something we call the Voice. Although we use the term the "Voice," you can use other words that are more comfortable for you. Some people call the Voice the enemy, the spoiler, the critic, etc. Within our church classes we (Pat and Terry) have found that calling the Voice the "Enemy" has been quite successful because many churches use that terminology to describe the darker side of human nature. Other names that people have suggested are: the Spoiler, the Nasty One, the Accuser, and the Adversary. If you would rather use one of these or some other name for what we call the "Voice," please feel free to do so. Whatever name you choose, your progress in learning these skills will be amplified by making the Voice as "real" as possible, even though it is simply a metaphor for that side of us that we would do better without.

This means you are the owner of your healthy thoughts; the Voice is the owner of the unhealthy thoughts. Everyone has a Voice. We only differ in how intense or frequent it is. There is just ONE Voice. You are the owner of all the good thoughts in your head. The Voice has only one goal: to run your life and make you miserable.

Because you are real and the Voice is imaginary, you will eventually defeat the Voice. The Voice always lies, even when it is not obvious. To defeat the Voice in your life, you must know it intimately. The Voice is a master magician. It is deceptive and sneaky.

Because of human imperfection, your thought life is negatively affected by the work of the Voice. No matter how well your life is going, the Voice continually tries to sabotage you. If you have you ever felt like someone else was living inside of you, then you have identified the Voice. If you have you ever felt as if you were not in control, then the Voice is in charge of your life.

You must never forget that the Voice wants you to believe that your struggles are really against yourself. The greatest deception it can ever perpetrate on you is to make you believe It doesn't exist. Remember, Christ was able to clearly hear and see the enemy (Voice). You can be more like Christ by being more aware of the Voice's presence.

Read the Voice Dossier aloud (see following page) every morning soon after waking. Some people find it helpful to make a copy of the Voice Dossier and tape it to the bathroom mirror.

Voice Dossier
Facts About the Voice.

1. The Voice always lies.
2. The Voice completely distorts reality.
3. The Voice hates change.
4. The Voice likes everything in black and white.
5. The Voice wants me to think I am worthless and powerless to change my life.
6. The Voice wants me to obey an unreasonable set of rules.
7. The Voice is repetitious, habitual and dull!
8. The Voice wants me to judge other people based on their behavior.
9. The Voice will use subtle messages to enslave me.
10. The Voice loves to make me feel obligated by using "should" words.
11. The Voice knows exactly what buttons to push with me.
12. The Voice is malicious, nasty and sneaky.
13. Everything the Voice says is logically flawed and, at best, a half truth.
14. Beware of the Voice's observation assumption trick. For example:
    a. *Observation*: Your friend didn't want to come over tonight.
    b. *Assumption*: That means you must have done something to hurt her feelings.
15. To agree with the Voice, no matter how reasonable it sounds, is to always be defeated.
16. The Voice wants me to get caught in an undertow of emotions, seemingly fighting myself around and around in circles.
17. The Voice's best weapons are secrecy and speed. I must expose it and slow it down.
18. The Voice is like the wizard in the Wizard of Oz: a tiny, frightened thing trying to get me to believe it is larger than life and quite terrifying.
19. The Voice uses illusion to put fear in the hearts of those who are stronger than it is.
20. The Voice wants to convince me that its cheap tricks are part of the real world.
21. The Voice is a coward! It loves hitting me when I'm down.
22. The Voice's only purpose in life is to survive.
23. If I am not actively fighting the Voice, I am automatically agreeing with its messages.
24. I need to anticipate times of stress because this is when the Voice will try to regain a foothold in my life.
25. Guilt is one of the Voice's tricks to keep me dependent upon the unrealistic expectations of other people.
26. The Voice wants me to be resentful so that I will eventually cut off all human support and caring.
27. The Voice is my worst enemy and wants me to be miserable.
28. The Voice likes to play it safe. The Voice is gutless!
29. The Voice tries to trick me by insisting that a low probability event has a good chance of happening.
30. When I take risks, I challenge the Voice. The Voice wants me to be immobilized with fear.

Pests In Your Garden

The Voice has many ways to destroy the garden of your mind. It can unleash a horde of pests (destructive thought patterns) that can easily destroy your fruit of the spirit. The Voice has many and varied pests to ruin your garden. You may not experience all of them, but you need to be aware of all of them. Here is a list of all the pests.

Black and White Bug
Life must be lived in the extremes, says the Voice. You must always see your day-to-day experiences as either-or. You are either happy or miserable, either a wonderful person or a rotten person. Viewing your relationships and the people involved as either "all this" or "all that" narrowly defines them as one-dimensional shadows, thereby demeaning them.

Blind Alley Bug
The Voice likes to send this bug when you have really important decisions to make. It wants you to believe you have only one good way to make a decision. It will appear that all of your good choices have evaporated.

Busy-Busy Bug
If the Voice can keep you running as fast as possible, it can keep your mind too occupied to listen to what it is saying. If you can't hear the Voice, then you can't defeat it.

Comparison Bug
This common mental pest is always comparing you with other people, but only in a way that shows you as inferior to others. Comparison bugs always keep you in a one-down position and you must vigorously oppose them.

Control Bug
This pest wants to drive you crazy by convincing you that you should be able to control the way other people behave. You can't control other people, no matter how hard you try; you are only in charge of yourself.

Demands Bug
The Voice likes to tell you what to do by bringing this bug into your garden. That's because the Voice's main goal is to run your life. The Demands Bug will make you feel like a slave, unable to make your own decisions and manage your own life.

Emotional Reasoning
Bug The Voice will try to get you to assume that what you feel is the absolute truth. For example, it may try to get you to believe that if you feel stupid, then you must be stupid. The truth is that you are a person who has feelings. It makes no sense to think that the feelings you have can define who you are as a person.

Exaggeration Bug
The more the Voice can exaggerate what happens in your life, the better chance it has of increasing your confusion. You can bet that most of what the Voice says to you is some type of exaggeration. You can spot this bug by listening for words such as "always," "never," "most," "forever."

Interpretation Bug
This is also a very common bug because our brain is continuously seeking to make sense of life. The Interpretation Bug allows the Voice to interpret your life for you.

Jump Ahead Bug
The Voice may initiate this bug by telling you that you are not learning this material fast enough. It wants you to go on quickly before you have mastered the present skills. If the Voice can infest your garden with enough of these bugs, your chances of failure increases—exactly what the Voice wants. You don't need to let this happen. Be patient.

Label Bug

By using this bug, the Voice forces you to deal with the world in a limited way. Labels, such as "stupid," "lazy," "incompetent," are self-limiting because they allow for no flexibility or change. Labels run us in circles and demean people while violating the principle of Christian love.

Magical Thinking Bug

One can easily spot this bug by the phrase "If . . . then . . ." Example: "If you would just be a better person, then you could get everybody to like you." The most dangerous toxin this bug can infect you with is the illusion that God is a Divine Santa Claus who will grant your every wish if you just "try hard enough to be a good Christian."

Mind-Reading Bug

This bug will pollute you with the silly notion that you can read another person's mind. Nobody can be certain that they know what someone else is thinking or feeling.

Myth of the Good Friend Bug

This bug's toxin has the opposite effect of the previous bug. This bug wants you to believe that the other person should be able to read your mind. When you allow this bug to stay in your garden, you set yourself up for feeling disappointed and rejected when another person does not respond to your suffering in silence.

Prediction Bug

Like the Mind-Reading Bug, this one fouls your brain by making convincing you that you can predict the future. Since most people are sincerely curious about the future, this bug is very easy for the Voice to sneak into your garden.

Silence Bug

As you get better at engaging the Voice, it will try to put the Silence Bug into your garden. It will try to fool you by remaining silent when you try to listen to its lies. If the Voice is silent, just guess what it might be saying to you. The practice is good for you and you will find that you are more often right than not.

Stereo Bug

One of the most amusing bugs for the Voice is the Stereo Bug. This is similar to listening to music through a set of headphones—you get different information in each ear. Regardless of which of the two messages you follow, the Voice wins because it is now running your life by telling you what to do.

Success Bug

As you become stronger and more successful in defeating the Voice, this bug may suddenly appear. The Voice will use this to discount your successes. This way your successes never become a part of your nature and remain detached and distant.

Surprise Bug

This bug will probably be with you for the rest of your life. No matter how often you swat it, it will come back. As you get more experienced, the Voice will be less and less able to surprise you. Remember this motto: Never Be Surprised by Surprises.

Why, Why, Why Bug

Normal human curiosity makes all of us susceptible to the bite of this bug. You will find life more prosperous when you begin to change each "why" question bug into a "what" and a "how" question. For example, instead of asking yourself why your best friend treated you badly, you can destroy this bug by asking yourself, "What did she do?" followed by, "How am I going to deal with it?"

Wishful Thinking Bug

This bug confuses wishing with expecting. Wishes are future events that have low probability; expectations are future events that have high probability. The Voice wants you to waste your time wishing for things rather than taking action to get your needs met.

Study the list of garden pests then begin to track them this next week by using the Pest Log. The first column is for identifying which pests are present in your garden right now. Spend time each night reviewing the list of bugs and identify which ones invaded your garden.

Pest Log

Pest Name	Mon	Tues	Wed		Fri	Sat	Sun
Black & White							
Blind Alley							
Busy-Busy							
Comparison							
Control							
Demands							
Either Or							
Emotional Reasoning							
Exaggeration							
Interpretations							
Jump Ahead							
Label							
Magical Thinking							
Mind Reading							
Myth of the Good Friend							
Predictions							
Silence							
Stereo							
Surprise							
Success							
Why, Why, Why							
Wishful Thinking							

Voice Exercise

In each of the examples below, these people behaved in ways they could not explain because they did not know about the Voice trying to run their lives. What could the Voice be telling them to drive their emotions and behaviors?

A man on a new strict diet, faithfully counting calories and exercising daily, suddenly, late at night, after a long day, pulls off the road at a convenience store and quickly devours 2 brownies, completely blowing his diet for the day.

Voice Messages Could Be:

A woman who is "on the wagon" because of a long history of alcohol abuse has a terrible day of kids talking back, her husband being verbally abusive and customers at work being mean to her. Finally, late at night, when no one is looking, she reaches into the cabinet. Knowing it is an unwise decision, she grabs a bottle of Vodka and takes several deep drinks directly from the bottle.

Voice Messages Could Be:

A man fighting a problem with verbal abuse and anger management has been to counseling and several weeks of courses. One day, after promising to never do it again, he rages at his 5 year old daughter, scaring her so badly she is terrified to the point of uncontrollable sobbing.

Voice Messages Could Be:

A woman with the responsibility of a large family to feed "sleeps in" on Christmas morning because she is so depressed. She misses the joy of watching her children open their presents and must live with her family being angry with her.

Voice Messages Could Be:

A man loses sleep almost every night. He wakes up in a cold sweat, panicky and breathing rapidly. Images of the pressures of the day ahead are racing through his mind. He finally falls asleep at dawn and oversleeps his alarm even though he knows his responsibilities are awaiting him.

Voice Messages Could Be:

An overweight teen skips her regularly scheduled exercise routine. She suddenly doesn't "feel like" going to the gym and has an internal struggle about the value of exercise.

Voice Messages Could Be:

A man calls his boss late at night because he is still furious about the harsh session he had at work listening to his boss review his yearly performance. He lets the boss have it, telling him what a no good S.O.B. he is.

Voice Messages Could Be:

Discussion Questions

1. How do the pests in your garden keep you from living the worry free life?

2. Read Matthew 6:28 where Jesus says that worry is a sin. How can ridding the pests from your garden help you clean sin out of your life?

3. The pests are often associated with specific life events. When you have gotten rid of the pests, what are some wholesome concerns you could have about these situations? For example, your daughter is leaving home for the first time. The Voice puts the Prediction Pest into your garden so you will worry about her daily life. If this were your situation, what would be some healthy concerns you might have about her living on her own?

4. Read Joel 2:25. Describe the quality of your life when you can destroy the pests in your garden.

5. Are you ready to make a commitment to learn the necessary skills to get rid of your garden's pests (you will learn these in the upcoming sessions)?

See chapter 4 in *The Worry Free Life* for more on the pests.

The Worry Free Life Session #5:
Routing Out the Vermin

Search me, O God, and know my heart; test me and know my thoughts.
— Psalm 139:23 (NLT)

Identifying the Vermin

According to George Lakoff, Professor of Cognitive Linguistics at UC Berkeley, 95% of what we think is "non-conscious." That means we are aware of only 5% of what we are thinking. Scientists call these non-conscious thoughts and beliefs "silent assumptions" and "automatic thoughts."

Our Voice is clever and deceitful. When you first take steps to expose it, it will try to hide. It will disguise it's lies. It knows you want to be free so it will try to change the subject, change the language, and even be silent. Its two favorite weapons are speed and secrecy.

Questioning the Voice is an unnatural thing to do. We usually don't like to pursue the unpleasant thoughts and the Voice counts on that. By going after the Voice with the following three tools, you will stay in control and eventually force it to give up one or more of the Vermin (keyword). Once that happens, you've begun to take your life back. We will discuss, in the following courses, how to fight back once you have the keyword, but for now, just practice interrogating until it quits. You can do this indefinitely which keeps you in control.

The vermin represent the most basic and destructive lies the Voice can use against you. Fortunately, there are only six of them. You may remember from lesson 3 that there are also only six toxic, destructive emotions. We will show you how the six vermin relate to the six toxic emotions in the next course. Your assignment this week will be to uncover these vermin by finding the keywords. The keywords represent the vermin (core lies) that we will cover in more detail in Session #6. For now, all we want you to do is merely identify the keywords. The six keywords are:

1. **Should**
2. **Worthless "them"**
3. **Danger**
4. **Stand**
5. **Worthless "Me"**
6. **Tragedy**

Keyword	Example
Should	You should not have bought those shoes.
Worthless (them)	Your neighbor is rude and disgusting—he is basically a worthless human being.
Danger	The panic you are feeling right is really dangerous and could seriously harm you.
Stand	You can't stand the way your children treat you.
Worthless (me)	You hurt your friend's feelings—that makes you worthless.
Tragedy	If your husband loses his job, your family will be homeless and that would be a tragedy.

In the table below, rate how strong these Keywords are in your life on a scale of 1-5 with 5 being the strongest.

Keyword	1	2	3	4	5
Should					
Worthless (them)					
Danger					
Stand					
Worthless (me)					
Tragedy					

Digging Deeper Into Your Writing

The Voice will hide its keywords in one of three ways. It will . . .

Make a *Statement*
Make a *Demand*
Ask a *Question*

To find the hidden keyword in these statements, demands, and questions, you will use a specific response for each non-keyword Voice utterance. If all you hear is silence after you use one of these responses, make something up! Because you are just learning the Interrogation Response, guessing will allow you to keep going when the Voice wants you to go away. The odd thing about guessing is that you will probably guess correctly at least 90% of the time.

For each of these hiding places you will use a different Interrogation Technique.

When the Voice makes a statement: you will answer: *"So what if you think...?"*
When the Voice makes a demand: you will answer: *"Why should I...?"*
When the Voice asks you a question: you will answer: *"It's none of your business!"*

Statement	So what if you think . . .
Demand	Why should I . . .
Question	It's none of your business!

Begin a 2-column Interrogation Diary.

- ◆ Write what the Voice says in the left column and write your response in the right column.
- ◆ Mediate on Psalm 139:23 and ask God to help you uncover the Voice's lies.
- ◆ Here is a sample Interrogation Diary.

Voice	Me
You hurt your friend's feelings.	So what if you think I hurt my friend's feelings? (this is so different than trying to defend yourself)
She will never talk to you again.	So what if you think she will never talk to me again?
Call her and apologize.	Why should I call her and apologize?
Don't you care if she ever talks to you again?	That's none of your business!
You'll be sorry.	So what if you think I'll be sorry?
You'll never be able to find that good of a friend.	So what if you think I will never be able to find that good of a friend?
That would be a tragedy.	Ha. Caught you. Tragedy is a keyword. (You would also circle the word tragedy in the column on your left)

Common Voice Messages

Read the following Common Voice Messages. Identify and mark all the messages you have ever heard from the Voice. Don't mark them based on whether you believe them or not, but rather on whether you have heard them. Mark an item even if you have only heard it once. Mark an item even if you only heard it a long time ago. Mark an item even if the Voice used different language that meant the same thing.

1. You have to be loved by someone or you will be miserable.
2. Making mistakes is terrible.
3. You are an awful human being.
4. It's terrible when things go wrong.
5. Your emotions can't be controlled.
6. You should really worry about scary situations.
7. Self-discipline is just too hard for you to achieve.
8. You're so weak, you have to depend on someone else.
9. Your childhood must always affect you.
10. You can't stand the way some people act.
11. Every problem has a perfect solution — so keep looking.
12. You should be better than others.
13. If someone criticizes you, you must have done something wrong.
14. You can't change the way you think.
15. You should help everyone who needs it.
16. You must never show any weakness.
17. Healthy people don't get upset.
18. There is one true love.
19. You should never hurt anyone.
20. There is a magic cure for your problems.
21. It's someone else's responsibility to solve your problems.
22. Strong people don't ask for help.
23. If something bad can happen, it probably will.
24. You can only do things when you feel like it — when you are in the mood.
25. You are inferior.
26. You are always in the spotlight — people keep watching you.
27. Some people ought to do what you wish.

28. Give up!
29. Change is awful.
30. Knowing how your problems started when you were young is essential.
31. Everybody should trust you.
32. If you're not happy, something is wrong with you.
33. There is a secret, terrible part of you that controls your life.
34. Working on your problems is too upsetting.
35. The world ought to be fair.
36. You are not responsible for what you do sometimes.
37. Some feelings are really dangerous.
38. You should be able to control another person's behavior.
39. If you just had enough will power, you would not have these problems.
40. You must always make the right decision.

You may remember that we told you the Voice always lies—even though these lies are not always obvious. You have just finished reading forty of the most common Voice lies. Your next task is to rewrite all forty of these lies on another sheet of paper. There are many different ways you can rewrite these lies. If you have any difficulties, you see how we changed these lies to truths later on in this session.

Finally, put a copy of the Common Voice Messages on your bathroom mirror and read them aloud each morning when you wake up. This will help you remember that the most important part of the day is to remember the Voice and hear what it is saying to you.

Say Goodbye to the Voice

Are you ready to say goodbye to the Voice once and for all? When something is no longer useful or valuable you usually get rid of it. The same is true of the Voice. Have you been holding on to the Voice because it tells you that something dreadful will happen if you get rid of it? This is just another stupid prediction trying to get you off its back. On the next page we have excerpts from some sample letters that others have written to the Voice. They were written by people who had decided they wanted to live life without the Voice's presence. They were tired of continually living with the restrictions put on them by the Voice.

When you have finished reading the samples, write a letter of your own to the Voice. It is okay to be sarcastic, rude or belligerent. When you have finished, read it over and decide whether you want to say farewell to a life of misery with the Voice as your constant companion. It you like the letter, post it where you can see it daily. You might even want to read it aloud to your Grace Partner or members of your study group. Some people become a poison pen-pal with the Voice and write a similar letter several times a week.

Sample Goodbye Letters to the Voice

Dear Voice:

Guess what — you are on your way out. I'm sick and tired of carrying you around. You've kept me from feeling good about myself, destroyed my self respect, messing up my life, keeping me from enjoying my family, friends and everything else I think freedom from you offers. I want a total life. Good riddance!

　　　Sincerely,

Dear Jerk:

Thank you for all you've done for me. My husband is absolutely thrilled that I can't go shopping at my favorite stores. The charge accounts are very low! You have made my life much simpler because I have no desire to show off my fears at parties and social gatherings. We don't need two cars anymore because I can't go anyplace even if I wanted to. And last but not least, my husband no longer cares what color my hair is because he doesn't seem to notice me anymore.

      Thanks a lot,

Goodbye Sucker:

You have finally shown your true colors and I see you for what you really are. I was not aware of it before, but others around me were. Frankly, you are very objectionable and I have decided that I can live without you. So bug off!!! You are no longer welcome in my life. These words may not seem polite or pretty, but that's the way it is. Voice, I have discovered your true colors and decided these colors clash with mine.

      Your Ex

Your Personal Poison Pen-Pal Letter to the Voice

Dear Voice: Date: _____

Thanks for all you have done for me all these years. . .

[Sign off] [Your name]

Here is a small quiz to see how well you can identify the Keywords. We have presented 12 mini-vignettes. Since there are six Keywords, you will find each Keyword twice. The legend tells you what the initials above each column stand for. The answers are on the next page.

Identifying Voice Keywords

> **Legend:**
>
> ST=Stand; SH=Should; WM=Worthless (me);
> WT=Worthless (them); TR=Tragedy; DA=Danger

	ST	SH	WM	WM	TR	DA	
1							Your mother is awful because she makes fun of you.
2							You're rotten because you cheated on your spouse ten years ago
3							It's really frightening when you feel depressed.
4							You just have to get over this problem of yours.
5							What a calamity if this airplane should crash—and you're so young
6							You shouldn't have hurt your friend's feelings like that.
7							You just can't tolerate your husband's stupid jokes.
8							It would be a catastrophe if you didn't get that job.
9							Anyone who commits a serious crime ought to be shot.
10							This anxiety is dangerous and could make you crazy.
11							You're a terrible person because your spouse left you and got custody of the kids.
12							This job is driving you up the wall.

Possible Truths to the 40 Voice Lies

1. *People must love you or you will be miserable.* The truth of the matter is that nobody has to love you—not even your own mother. It would be nice if everybody did love you, but there are no guarantees that anybody will. "Must" is an absolute word which puts pressure on you to be perfect and to feel guilty if you're not. The Voice is telling you that you must do everything in your power to get people to love you or you will be a miserable person. This is unrealistic and you could never hope to achieve this impossible goal.

2. *Making mistakes is terrible.* The word "terrible" is a complete exaggeration. Making mistakes is inconvenient and human! You cannot learn from them if you think they are catastrophic. You only sink more deeply and spin your wheels trying to be "more perfect."

3. *You are an awful human being.* Another totally unrealistic statement by the Voice. You are not an awful human being. You are the sum total of all your life experiences. Though you may think you've done some pretty awful things, these things are not what you are. This is a judgmental statement indicating that people are either good or bad.

4. *It is terrible when things go wrong.* You may feel uncomfortable or anxious when things do not go as planned, but it is not "terrible." Life has lots of unpredictability. That's what makes it so fascinating. The word "terrible" sets up a state of panic in your mind—just what the Voice wants. The minute you start feeling how "terrible" everything is, you start feeling hopeless. The Voice likes hopelessness.

5. *Your emotions cannot be controlled.* This is untrue, as you will find out when you learn to defeat the Voice. "Can't" expresses helplessness. You can control your emotions by controlling the Voice. The Voice is what triggers your destructive emotions.

6. You should really be worried about threatening situations. The words "you should" reveal a strong outside influence dictating and judging your actions. That strong outside influence is the Voice. You can be concerned, but you don't have to be worried. Worrying accomplishes nothing. Threatening situations are uncomfortable but worrying about them only makes them worse.

7. *Self-discipline is too hard for you to achieve.* "Too" is the key word here. Self-discipline can be very difficult at times, but it is not impossible to achieve. It takes perseverance and lots of repetitive, hard work. The Voice is trying to set you up for another failure so you'll not even begin your personal improvement program.

8. *You must depend on other people.* There's that word "must" again, putting pressure on you to give up your independent thinking by always depending on others believe what is "right," "wrong," "good," or "bad." Listen to yourself and learn to depend on yourself. The Voice wants you to think you are helpless and can't do anything for yourself. God has given you intelligence and a good mind.

9. *Your childhood must always affect you.* Pure nonsense! Yes, your childhood has much to do with who you are now, but it need not affect the way you run your life in the here-and- now. You can transcend your childhood. The first step is to recognize some of the things that happened in your childhood, forgive your parents, others, and yourself for being less than perfect, and then go on with your life. Forgiveness is the key, which we will cover in course #9.

10. *You just can't stand the way some people act.* Another exaggeration! Some of the things that people do and say will annoy you. The Voice, however, is trying to tell you these people are the sum total of all their faults and annoying ways. The Voice is asking you to expect perfection from other fallible human beings.

11. *Every problem has a perfect solution.* There is no such thing as the "perfect solution." If you expect to wait and wait until you eventually find the perfect solution, you will take forever to solve the problem at hand. There is no pot of gold at the end of the rainbow. You will also set yourself up for failure by expecting to find the perfect solution.

12. *You should be better than others.* There's that strong outside influence again (the Voice)—the one that dictates to you and judges you. Why should you be better than others? Because the Voice tells you that you should be? Ridiculous! This statement is unreasonable. You don't expect others to be better than you, do you? The Voice is asking you to constantly compare yourself to other people. Just be yourself and let others be themselves.

13. *If others criticize you, you must have done something wrong.* You may have believed this one for a long time. This statement is similar to "If you do things that are bad, you are bad." Another total lie. Remember, others may find fault with you for reasons stemming from their own insecurities. Also, the word "wrong" is needlessly judgmental.

14. *You can't change what you think*. This is the only thing you really can change, so the statement is a complete untruth. The Voice is trying to keep you locked up in your misery. Remember, "can't" denotes helplessness. Say instead, "I want to change what I think, even though it will require lots of work." This makes the task a very real possibility.

15. *You should help everyone who needs it*. The Voice is saying you are responsible for the needs of everyone around you. You can't please all of the people all of the time. You can't be all things to all people. It is good to be helpful and to be thoughtful, but not at the expense of forgetting to take care of yourself. Besides, you don't have the capacity to help everyone, and people have to want to have help anyway. The Voice is trying to make you feel guilty if you fail at helping everyone. Just do the best you can.

16. *You must never show any weakness*. This statement is loaded with untruths, even though you may have believed it all your life. "You must" denotes that you absolutely have to be perfect no matter what. "You must" never gives you any room at all for error. "You must never show any" says that all weakness is bad. Weakness is a very human and compassionate quality. Strong people are often the only people who are capable of admitting they have any weaknesses. You need to have weakness in order to have strength.

17. *Healthy people don't get upset*. The Voice is telling that if you were only free of problems and therefore perfect, you would automatically become serene and calm. The truth is, healthy people allow themselves to get upset from time to time. They know there is nothing wrong with it, that it will not lead to insanity. They have effective ways of dealing with turmoil and are able to feed themselves constructive thoughts which then generate constructive emotions. Getting upset is not bad.

18. *There is one true love*. Many people really do want to believe this. You may not like the fact that it isn't true. The truth is that love is a human emotion and therefore fallible. Besides, one person isn't capable of fulfilling all the needs of another person. This myth places extra, unnecessary pressure on the one being loved. He or she must never fail being the "true love" whom you have labeled. In the same regard, don't think that you need to be a perfect, true lover, either. It just isn't possible. You can love any number of people in your life, but making the relationship succeed is a matter of commitment and hard work. It isn't a matter of finding the "perfect" mate.

19. *You should never hurt anyone*. Those wonderful words "should" and "never" again. They certainly don't leave any room for doubt, do they? Not hurting people is good in theory, but people will get their feelings hurt, even if you do not mean to hurt them. Sometimes when you stand up for yourself and are truthful about your feelings, another person might view it as rejection and feel hurt. Remember, though, people have to allow themselves to be hurt.

20. *There is a magic cure for your problems*. The Voice is trying to get you to believe that one morning you are going to wake up and find you are cured of all problems and perfectly in control. Obviously, this won't happen. You need to work on your problems every day and face them realistically.

21. *It's someone else's responsibility to solve your problems*. The Voice wants you to think you are incapable of solving your own problems, that you are helpless and must have someone else do all the work and give you the answers. But really it is your responsibility. You can ask for guidance and for suggestions from others, but ultimately, you have to make the commitment to change.

22. *Strong people don't ask for help*. Another variation of "It's weak, and therefore bad, to need help." The truth is, strong people ask for help when they need it because they know there is no shame in needing help. Actually, the stronger you are, the more likely you are to ask for help. You know both your strengths and your weaknesses and accept yourself as being human. The Voice is telling you another wearisome untruth.

23. *You can do things only when you're in the mood*. This one is very familiar. You may think that if you put something off because you're not in the mood, the time will come when you are in the mood to do it. Another variation is, "You can relax only when you're in the mood to relax." The opposite is true. You need to learn how to relax when you're not in the mood. The Voice is giving you excuses for your avoidance of responsibility to yourself.

24. *Possible is the same as probable*. "It is possible that my guests will think I'm a terrible housekeeper" translates into "My guests will think I'm a terrible housekeeper." This is a typical Voice statement. Ninety-nine percent of all the predictions the Voice makes never happen.

25. *You are inferior*. Of course you are not inferior! You may think at times that you are inferior, but that is because you are listening to the Voice without evaluating what it is saying to you. You have a right to your lifestyle and your choices in life. Making mistakes doesn't make you inferior.

You are no better or no worse than the next person. The Voice wants you to feel subservient and victimized by the demands of others. The irony here is that the Voice is telling you that you are inferior in one ear while telling you that you must be better than others (the Stereo Bug) in the other ear.

26. *You are always in the spotlight.* Or: "everyone is watching you all the time, so you'd better not screw up." The truth is, people are usually too concerned about themselves and their own problems to spend time watching you.

27. *People ought to do what you want them to.* The Voice is telling you that your wishes are more important than those of other people. Everyone's needs are personal and equal. By wishing correct behavior from other people, you automatically judge what they are doing. You don't want them judging you, do you? Besides, you can't wish people into doing anything. Live and let live.

28. *Giving up is the best policy.* The Voice loves this one. It's so easy to throw up your hands and say, "I can't. I quit." When you do this, you give the Voice complete dominance over your life. When you give up, the Voice has the perfect opportunity to feed you all kinds of destructive messages. Instead of quitting, work harder at feeding yourself constructive thoughts.

29. *Change is awful.* Change can be painful because the consequences are often unknown, but it is not awful. Change can give you new opportunities to grow and learn. Change keeps your mind open and your life from becoming stagnant.

30. *Knowing how your problems started when you were young is essential.* It's good to have perspective and to find out what started you on your roller coaster ride into destructive behavior, but it is not essential. What is essential is that you start now by changing how you think. Besides, you can't change what happened when you were young. Everyone around you probably did the best they could with what information they had at the time. You probably did the best you could do. Remember: forgive yourself and others.

31. *Everybody should trust you.* Trust is something that is earned and cannot be considered a "should." People often have their own built-in mistrust. Don't let that bother you. Just concentrate on being trustworthy to yourself and the rest will come in time if you are patient. Be true to yourself.

32. *If you are not happy, something is wrong with you.* This just isn't possible for any human being. The Voice is trying to make you feel guilty if you aren't "Little Miss Sunny Skies" every day of your life. You'll always have your down days. This is just part of life. Without some sadness, there certainly wouldn't be any happiness. Being a "full" human being involves both.

33. *There is a secret, terrible part of you that controls your life.* The Voice wants you to think you are a slave to some kind of "evil" force within you. The truth of the matter is this "secret" thing within has been the Voice all along and you just didn't know it. You have been a slave to the destructive emotions the Voice has been giving you. You have forgotten to look for the "good" qualities you possess. There is no terrible part of you. I know you've thought that for a long time, but it's just the Voice trying to stop you from believing that you are in control of your life.

34. *Working on your problems is scary.* For you, diving into the deep murky waters of your being might be scary. Fortunately, "scary" has never harmed anyone. Working on yourself is very rewarding, especially when you begin to see results. Working on your problems is a challenge. By saying that "working on your problems is scary," the Voice wants you to be overwhelmed by all the supposed obstacles in your path to recovery.

35. *The world ought to be fair.* Maybe it ought to be, but it isn't! That's just a fact of life. Remember, you cannot change the world you live in or the people in it. But you can change how you perceive the world, how you perceive others, and how you perceive yourself.

36. *You are not responsible for what you do sometimes.* As a thinking adult with the power of choice, you are responsible for your behavior. The Voice wants you to remain a child forever—blaming everyone and everything except yourself for the way you act. Condemning yourself, however, is worthless because it robs you of the energy you need to take positive action. You are not responsible for another person's feelings, either—just for your own actions and behavior toward others. If you have behaved in such a way as to violate someone's rights, the only remedy is action on your part. You can rectify the situation by offering an apology and doing something to make restitution.

37. *Anxiety is always dangerous.* Anxiety cannot hurt you. Anxiety is nothing more than an exaggerated physical reaction related to normal feelings. You can tolerate moderate anxiety by realizing that healthy anxiety will improve your ability to handle any situation. Extreme anxiety can be very stressful, but this stress can be reduced by doing your stress reduction exercises such as natural breathing, deep muscle relaxation, and mind calming. You also need to realize the Voice is

trying to make everything much worse than it really is. Not only does moderate anxiety not hurt you, it gives you the warning signal to let go of the stress which has been building up in your life.

38. *You should be able to control another person's behavior.* The Voice is giving you another guilty "should." You can't do anything about another person's behavior—only about your own. You are also not responsible for another person's behavior. If you see that someone is upset about something, you may automatically assume that you must have done something to make that person upset or that you could have in some way prevented him or her from being upset. Once again, the Voice lies.

39. *Willpower alone can solve your problems.* "If you just had enough willpower. . ." How many times has the Voice—and others—said that to you? Well, the Voice knows that you, like most people, have enough willpower. If it can get you to believe willpower is your missing ingredient to a better life, it will lead you into a blind alley. The real issue is not lack of willpower but lack of effective coping skills, such as getting the Voice out of your life.

40. *You must always make the right decision.* If you always made the right decision, nothing would be challenging anymore. God put us here on this earth to learn from our mistakes. Also, there are no "right" and "wrong" decisions. These are judgmental words the Voice uses to make you feel guilty. Don't condemn yourself for not always being right.

Discussion Questions

1. What have you learned about having a Grace partner?

2. Discuss the effectiveness of Voice Interrogation for finding the Voice's Keywords.

3. Which keywords are the most common ones the Voice uses in your life?

4. Describe how these Keywords are the source of misery and unhappiness for you.

For more information on Voice Interrogation, see chapter 5 in *The Worry Free Life*.

The Worry Free Life
Session #6: Putting It All Together

Carefully guard your thoughts because they are the source of true life.
—Proverbs 4:23 (CEV)

All the information from previous chapters can be understood using the Dominoes metaphor. For each metaphor chain below give an example from your own life.

Domino Exercise

Mistake ⇨ Broke a Rule ⇨ Guilt ⇨ Self-punishment ⇨ Another Mistake

Think of a time when you made a mistake:

What was it?

What did the Voice say to you?

Describe the guilt. How bad was it?

How did you punish yourself?

Describe how that was another mistake.

Violate You ⇨ Worthless (them) ⇨ Resentment ⇨ Violate the Violator

Think of a time when someone violated your rights:

What was the violation?

What did the Voice tell you?

How did the resentment feel?

Did you retaliate? How?

How did your actions violate the other person's rights?

Strong Feelings ⇨ This is Dangerous ⇨ Irrational Fear ⇨ Insulation ⇨ Stronger Feelings

Think of a time when your feelings felt dangerous.

What were the strong feelings?

What did the Voice tell you about these feelings?

Describe the irrational fear.

How did you withdraw or insulate yourself?

What happened to the strong feelings?

Loss ⇨ Worthless (me) ⇨ Depression ⇨ Lifelessness ⇨ More Loss

Think of a time when you were depressed.

What loss did you experience?

What did the Voice tell you?

Describe the depression?

How were you lifeless? For how long?

How did the depression contribute to more loss?

Conflict ⇨ Can't Stand It ⇨ Helplessness ⇨ Escape ⇨ Continued Conflict

Think of a time when you felt helpless or trapped.

What was the conflict? Was it internal or external?

What was the Voice telling you?

Describe the sense of helplessness.

What did you run away from?

Prediction ⇨ Tragedy ⇨ Unhealthy Anxiety ⇨ Avoidance ⇨ Prediction Remains

Think of a time when you felt unhealthy anxiety.

What was the threat?

What dire predictions was the Voice making?

Describe the unhealthy anxiety.

Did the prediction come true? Why not?

Your Truth Diary

Update your Interrogation Diary to a Truth Diary. Continue to interrogate the Voice using the 2-column format. This time, when you find the keyword, write the associated truth in the right column. An example of this might look like is on the next page.

Voice	Me
You hurt your friend's feelings.	So what if you think I hurt my friend's feelings? (this is so different than trying to defend yourself) [Statement]
She will never talk to you again.	So what if you think she will never talk to me again? [Statement]
Call her an apologize.	Why should I call her an apologize? [Demand]
Don't you care if she ever talks to you again?	That's none of your business! [Question]
You'll be sorry.	So what if you think I'll be sorry? [Statement]
You'll never be able to find that good of a friend.	So what if you think I will never be able to find that good of a friend? [Statement]
That would be a tragedy.	No matter what happens to me, I can respond as a mature, responsible adult. [Keyword: Tragedy]
You're not a responsible adult. You are rotten and good for nothing.	No matter what I do, I still have infinite worth. [Truth]
You can't stand not talking to your friend.	I've been standing it all my life. [Truth]
You shouldn't have treated her like that.	I can make my own decisions because I am a responsible adult. [Truth]
This guilt and depression you feel right now is destroying you.	Even though these feelings are uncomfortable they can make me stronger. [Truth]
Since your "friend" has let such a little thing come between you means she is despicable and unworthy of your friendship.	No matter what she does to me, she has infinite worth. [Truth]

At this point, you don't have to believe the Truth, you just need to understand it. The Voice will tell you that "you can't write the truth because you don't believe it." As with everything the Voice says, this is backward and untrue. The truth is that you won't believe it until you write it — often.

Discussion Questions

1. Are any of the truths difficult for you to believe? Talk about this with your study group or Grace Partner.

2. Which truths do you think will be the most helpful for you? Why?

3. Why does the Voice not want you to believe these truths?

4. What are some Bible verses you can use to help you believe and accept the truths?

The Worry Free Life
Session #7: Five Steps Towards Grace

Summing it all up, friends, I'd say you'll do best by filling your minds and meditating on things true, noble, reputable, authentic, compelling, gracious—the best, not the worst; the beautiful, not the ugly; things to praise, not things to curse.
— Philippians 4:8 (MSG)

Fighting the Voice

You have finally come to the point where you will put all your previous skills together to begin learning how to take your life back from the Voice. Once you identify the keyword, this process uses five consecutive steps:

Step #1:   Identify the Emotion
Step #2:   Name the Behavior
Step #3:   Repeat the Voice's Message
Step #4:   State the Truth
Step #5:   Argue, Argue, Argue

Examples

Voice: You should have gone to church yesterday.
You:
Step #1: Voice, you're trying to make me feel guilty.
Step #2: You want me to punish myself.
Step #3: You're telling me I should have gone to church yesterday
Step #4: The truth is I can make my own decisions because I am a responsible adult.
Step #5:
 · I am going to substitute the words "will" or "choose" for the word "should".
 · I am an adult and can decide for myself what is right and wrong.
 · I now realize that I only feel guilty when you try to confuse fantasy and reality.

You can add a Bible verse from the lists immediately after the Voice Fighting Road Map.

Voice: Your husband is contemptible because of what he did to you.
You:
Step #1: Voice, you're trying to make me feel resentment towards my husband.
Step #2: You want me to retaliate against him.
Step #3: You're telling me he is worthless because of what he did to me.
Step #4: The truth is no matter what he did to me he is still an infinitely worthwhile person.
Step #5:
 · Voice, you only want me to be resentful so that I will eventually cut off all human support and caring.
 · You lie when you tell me, Voice, that the way to get things done with other people is to retaliate so they won't hurt me again.
 · All of these resentful feelings are really making me weak and not strong as you would have me believe, Voice.

Voice: If your mother dies of cancer, you will be all alone and that would be a tragedy.
You:
Step #1: Voice, you're trying to make me feel unhealthy anxiety.

Step #2: You want me to avoid dealing with my mother's health.
Step #3: You're telling me it will be a tragedy when my mother eventually dies.
Step #4: The truth is nothing can happen which will keep me from making choices.
Step #5:
- It is reasonable to say "what if"; it is not reasonable to anticipate a personal tragedy or catastrophe.
- Even if something bad does happen, I can still act as a mature, responsible adult.
- I have always performed well and always will perform well in a crisis.

Voice: This grief you have been feeling is dangerous because it is destroying your sanity.
You:
Step #1: Voice, you're trying to make me feel irrational fear.
Step #2: You want me to insulate myself.
Step #3: You're telling me that feeling intense grief can destroy me.
Step #4: The Truth is even though these feelings are uncomfortable they can make me stronger.
Step #5:
- Feelings cannot destroy anyone—especially me.
- I refuse to let you, Voice, get me so irrationally afraid that I cannot think.
- I am tired of being afraid of things that cannot hurt me.

Voice: You just can't take it anymore. Your neighbor is so mean to your children.
You:
Step #1: Voice, you're trying to make me feel helpless.
Step #2: You want me to run away.
Step #3: You're telling me I can't stand the way my neighbor treats my children.
Step #4: The Truth is I have been standing it all my life.
Step #5:
- I may not like it, but I can deal with it.
- Agreeing with you, Voice, will only make me feel more powerless and miserable.
- If I run away from this situation now, things will only get worse and I will allow you, Voice to have more power over my life.

Voice: Your lack of commitment to your faith proves you are a worthless human being.
You:
Step #1: Voice, you're making me feel depressed.
Step #2: You want me to become lifeless.
Step #3: You're telling me I am worthless because my faith is not strong enough.
Step #4: The Truth is no matter what I do, I still have infinite worth.
Step #5:
- No one or nothing can make me feel depressed—only agreeing with you, Voice, can do that.
- I allow myself to feel depressed by agreeing with you, Voice, when you tell me that I am a no-good person.
- By keeping me depressed, you have total control over me—I refuse to allow this to happen!

On the next page you can see what the above would look like in the now familiar 2-column format. You need to follow this format for your own Voice Fighting Diary. When you have written many, many pages, you can eventually begin to Voice Fight verbally and then eventually mentally If you try mental Voice Fighting too soon, you will likely fail and then the Voice will get the upper hand.

Voice	Helen
How dare he try to explain this away after all you have done for him.	So what if I have done a lot for him?
Why did you marry such a man?	It is none of your business.
He will never change.	So what if he never changes?
He always does this to you.	So what if he always does this to me?
You should really let him have it.	Hah! That's the "should" keyword. 1. Voice, you're trying to get me to feel guilty. 2. You just want me to punish myself. 3. You are lying when you tell me that I should let him have it. 4. Well, the Truth is that I am a responsible adult and can make my own decision. 5. Argue, Argue, Argue · I am going to substitute the words "will" or "choose" for the word "should." · I am an adult and can decide for myself what is right and wrong. · Guilt is one of your tricks to keep me dependent upon the unrealistic expectations of other people. *Scripture*: The steps of the godly are directed by the LORD. He delights in every detail of their lives. Though they stumble, they will not fall, for the LORD holds them by the hand. [See next pages for a variety of possible Scripture verses]

The Voice Fighting Road Map

The next page has an enlarged version of Voice Fighting Road Map in *The Worry Free Life* book. Feel free to copy it

Next, you need to construct and use your Pest Control Kit. This puts all the steps for fighting the Voice in the palm of your hand. You can either make your own or order one from our web site: www.TheWorryFreeLife.com

The Pest Control Kit is the most important aide you will have for the rest of your life. You must use it to cheat whenever you need to fight the Voice. To master the skill of Voice Fighting you will probably want to practice hourly for about a week.

Convert your 2-column Truth Diary to a 2-column Voice Fighting Diary. Keep interrogating the Voice to find the keywords. When you find the keyword, use your Five Steps Towards Grace to find the Voice. The more pages you can do per week, the better prepared you will be to continue with the rest of this study guide.

This skill is, by far, the most important one in the entire book and Study Guide. All the pages prior to this have prepared you for this skill. All the following pages will help make the skill more powerful. Do you want to know The Secret? Voice Fighting is the secret to a happy Christian life! Bible Verses for Fighting Back.

Voice Fighting Road Map

What is the Voice saying?

Is there a keyword?

N → **Y**

1. **Emotion**
2. **Behavior**
3. **Message**
4. **Truth**
5. **Argue x 3**

STOP

Is the Voice still hassling you?

N ↑

Is it a statement? — **Y** →

"So what if you think...?"

N

Is it a demand? — **Y** →

"Why should I...?"

N

It is a question!

"It's none of your business"

Is the Voice repeating itself?

N

Y

Use canned phrase 3 times

Ignore the Voice

1. Distraction
2. Replanting

Bible Verses for Fighting Back

The best way to fight the Voice is with the truth—God's truth. Here are just a few of God's truths to help you when you argue (step #5) with the Voice. Use these as a starting off point and add to them when you can. It helps if you can memorize one key verse for each Keyword. This will give you something to fight with.

Should [Guilt]

And as far as sunrise is from sunset, he has separated us from our sins.
—Psalm 103:12 (MSG)
Once again you will have compassion on us. You will trample our sins under your feet and throw them into the depths of the ocean!
—Micah 7:19 (NLT)
For God made Christ, who never sinned, to be the offering for our sin, so that we could be made right with God through Christ.
—2 Corinthians 5:21 (NLT)
The steps of the godly are directed by the LORD. He delights in every detail of their lives. Though they stumble, they will not fall, for the LORD holds them by the hand.
—Psalm 37:23-24 (NLT)
Help, GOD—the bottom has fallen out of my life! Master, hear my cry for help! Listen hard! Open your ears! Listen to my cries for mercy. If you, GOD, kept records on wrongdoings, who would stand a chance? As it turns out, forgiveness is your habit, and that's why you're worshiped. I pray to GOD – my life a prayer – and wait for what he'll say and do. My life's on the line before God, my Lord, waiting and watching till morning, waiting and watching till morning. O Israel, wait and watch for GOD – with GOD's arrival comes love, with God's arrival comes generous redemption. No doubt about it – he'll redeem Israel, buy back Israel from captivity to sin.
—Psalm 130 (MSG)
I've seen it all in my brief and pointless life—here a good person cut down in the middle of doing good, there a bad person living a long life of sheer evil. So don't knock yourself out being good, and don't go overboard being wise. Believe me, you won't get anything out of it. But don't press your luck by being bad, either. And don't be reckless. Why die needlessly? It's best to stay in touch with both sides of an issue. A person who fears God deals responsibly with all of reality, not just a piece of it.
—Ecclesiastes 7:15-18 (MSG)
All that passing laws against sin did was produce more lawbreakers. But sin didn't, and doesn't, have a chance in competition with the aggressive forgiveness we call grace. When it's sin versus grace, grace wins hands down.
—Romans 5:20 (MSG)
God put the world square with himself through the Messiah, giving the world a fresh start by offering forgiveness of sins. God has given us the task of telling everyone what he is doing.
—2 Corinthians 5:19 (MSG)

Worthless (them) [Resentment]

Don't repay evil for evil. Don't retaliate when people say unkind things about you. Instead, pay them back with a blessing. That is what God wants you to do, and he will bless you for it.
—1 Peter 3:9 (NLT)
For God is pleased with you when, for the sake of your conscience, you patiently endure unfair treatment.
—1 Peter 2:19 (NLT)
Make a clean break with all cutting, backbiting, and profane talk. Be gentle with one another, sensitive. Forgive one another as quickly and thoroughly as God in Christ forgave you.
—Ephesians 4:31 (MSG)
GOD's now at my side and I'm not afraid; who would dare lay a hand on me? GOD's my strong champion; I flick off my enemies like flies.
—Psalm 118:6-7 (MSG)

Quick-tempered leaders are like mad dogs—cross them and they bite your head off. It's a mark of good character to avert quarrels, but fools love to pick fights.
—Proverbs 20:2-3 (MSG)
Don't let evil get the best of you, but conquer evil by doing good.
—Romans 12:21 (NLT)
If you set a trap for others, you will get caught in it yourself. If you roll a boulder down on others, it will roll back and crush you.
—Proverb 26:27 (NLT)
*A stone is heavy and sand is weighty, but the resentment caused by a fool is heavier than both. —Proverbs 27:3 (NLT)
There's far more to this life than trusting in Christ. There's also suffering for him. And the suffering is as much a gift as the trusting.
—Philippians 1:27-29 (MSG) Go ahead and be angry. You do well to be angry—but don't use your anger as fuel for revenge. And don't stay angry. Don't go to bed angry. Don't give the Devil that kind of foothold in your life.
—Ephesians 4:26 (MSG)

Danger [Irrational Fear]

The LORD is my light and my salvation—so why should I be afraid? The LORD protects me from danger so why should I tremble?
—Psalm 27:1 (NLT)
The LORD is my shepherd; I have everything I need. He lets me rest in green meadows; he leads me beside peaceful streams. He renews my strength. He guides me along right paths, bringing honor to his name. Even when I walk through the dark valley of death, I will not be afraid, for you are close beside me. Your rod and your staff protect and comfort me. You prepare a feast for me in the presence of my enemies. You welcome me as a guest, anointing my head with oil. My cup overflows with blessings. Surely your goodness and unfailing love will pursue me all the days of my life, and I will live in the house of the LORD forever.
—Psalm 23 (NLT)
The LORD's Covenant of Peace: "I will make a covenant of peace with them and drive away the dangerous animals from the land. Then my people will be able to camp safely in the wildest places and sleep in the woods without fear.
—Ezekiel 34:25 (NLT)
You will keep in perfect peace him whose mind is steadfast, because he trusts in you.
—Isaiah 26:3 (NLT)
The fruit of righteousness will be peace; the effect of righteousness will be quietness and confidence forever.
—Isaiah 32:17 (NLT)
"Do not fear, O Jacob my servant; do not be dismayed, O Israel. I will surely save you out of a distant place, your descendants from the land of their exile. Jacob will again have peace and security, and no one will make him afraid.
—Jeremiah 46:27 (NLT)
I will make a covenant of peace with them; it will be an everlasting covenant. I will establish them and increase their numbers, and I will put my sanctuary among them forever.
—Ezekiel 37:26 (NLT) Such people will not be overcome by evil circumstances. Those who are righteous will be long remembered. They do not fear bad news; they confidently trust the LORD to care for them. They are confident and fearless and can face their foes triumphantly.
—Psalm 112:6-8 (NLT)
Do not fear anything except the LORD Almighty. He alone is the Holy One. If you fear him, you need fear nothing else.
—Isaiah 8:13 (NLT)
So do not fear, for I am with you; do not be dismayed, for I am your God. I will strengthen you and help you; I will uphold you with my righteous right hand.
—Isaiah 41:10 (NIV)
For I am the LORD, your God, who takes hold of your right hand and says to you, Do not fear; I will help you.
—Isaiah 41:13 (NIV)

Stand [Helpless]

Our ancestors trusted in you, and you rescued them. You heard their cries for help and saved them. They put their trust in you and were never disappointed. . . Yet you brought me safely from my mother's womb and led me to trust you when I was a nursing infant. I was thrust upon you at my birth. You have been my God from the moment I was born.
—Psalm 22:4-10 (NLT)

Bless the LORD, who is my rock. He gives me strength for war and skill for battle.
—Psalm 144:1 (NLT)

We can rejoice, too, when we run into problems and trials, for we know that they are good for us—they help us learn to endure. And endurance develops strength of character in us, and character strengthens our confident expectation of salvation.
—Romans 5:3-4 (NLT)

They attacked me at a moment when I was weakest, but the LORD upheld me.
—Psalm 18:18 (NLT)

He lifted me out of the pit of despair, out of the mud and the mire. He set my feet on solid ground and steadied me as I walked along.
—Psalm 40:2 (NLT)

He gives power to those who are tired and worn out; he offers strength to the weak. Even youths will become exhausted, and young men will give up. But those who wait on the LORD will find new strength. They will fly high on wings like eagles. They will run and not grow weary. They will walk and not faint.
—Isaiah 40:29-30 (NLT)

For I can do everything with the help of Christ who gives me the strength I need.
—Philippians 4 (NLT)

But the people who know their God will be strong and will resist him.
—Daniel 11:32 (NLT)

Each time he said, "My gracious favor is all you need. My power works best in your weakness." So now I am glad to boast about my weaknesses, so that the power of Christ may work through me. —2 Corinthians 12:9 (NLT)

So if you are suffering according to God's will, keep on doing what is right, and trust yourself to the God who made you, for he will never fail you.
—1 Peter 4:19 (NLT)

By faith these people overthrew kingdoms, ruled with justice, and received what God had promised them. They shut the mouths of lions, quenched the flames of fire, and escaped death by the edge of the sword. Their weakness was turned to strength. They became strong in battle and put whole armies to flight.
—Hebrews 11:33-34 (NLT)

But you belong to God, my dear children. You have already won your fight with these false prophets, because the Spirit who lives in you is greater than the spirit who lives in the world.
—1 John 4:4 (NLT)

Worthless (me) [Depression]

Why are you down in the dumps, dear soul? Why are you crying the blues? Fix my eyes on God— soon I'll be praising again. He puts a smile on my face. He's my God.
—Psalm 43:5 (MSG)

Therefore, since we have been made right in God's sight by faith, we have peace with God because of what Jesus Christ our Lord has done for us.
—Romans 5:1 (NLT)

My dear children, you come from God and belong to God. You have already won a big victory over those false teachers, for the Spirit in you is far stronger than anything in the world.
—1 John 4:4 (MSG)

But there's one other thing I remember, and remembering, I keep a grip on hope: GOD's loyal love couldn't have run out, his merciful love couldn't have dried up. They're created new every morning. How great your faithfulness! I'm sticking with GOD (I say it over and over). He's all I've got left.
—Lamentations 3:21-24 (MSG)

It stands to reason, doesn't it, that if the alive-and-present God who raised Jesus from the dead moves into your life, he'll do the same thing in you that he did in Jesus, bringing you alive to himself? When God lives and breathes in you (and he does, as surely as he did in Jesus), you are delivered from that dead life. With his Spirit living in you, your body will be as alive as Christ's!
—Romans 8:11 (MSG)
Christ redeemed us from that self-defeating, cursed life by absorbing it completely into himself. Do you remember the Scripture that says, "Cursed is everyone who hangs on a tree"? That is what happened when Jesus was nailed to the Cross: He became a curse, and at the same time dissolved the curse. And now, because of that, the air is cleared and we can see that Abraham's blessing is present and available for non-Jews, too. We are all able to receive God's life, his Spirit, in and with us by believing—just the way Abraham received it.
—Galatians 3:13-14 (MSG)
And I am convinced that nothing can ever separate us from his love. Death can't, and life can't. The angels can't, and the demons can't. Our fears for today, our worries about tomorrow, and even the powers of hell can't keep God's love away.
—Romans 8:38 (NLT)
What can we say about such wonderful things as these? If God is for us, who can ever be against us?
—Romans 8:31 (NLT)
When I look at the night sky and see the work of your fingers—the moon and the stars you have set in place—what are mortals that you should think of us, mere humans that you should care for us? For you made us only a little lower than God, and you crowned us with glory and honor. You put us in charge of everything you made, giving us authority over all things
—Psalm 8:3-6 (NLT)
But whoever did want him, who believed he was who he claimed and would do what he said, He made to be their true selves, their child-of-God selves.
—John 1:12 (MSG) To the church of God which is at Corinth, to those who are sanctified in Christ Jesus, called to be saints, with all who in every place call on the name of Jesus Christ our Lord, both theirs and ours.
—1 Corinthians 1:2 (NKJV)
Paul, an apostle of Jesus Christ by the will of God, To the saints who are in Ephesus, and faithful in Christ Jesus.
—Ephesians 1:1 (NKJV) Paul and Timothy, bondservants of Jesus Christ, To all the saints in Christ Jesus who are in Philippi, with the bishops and deacons
—Philippians 1:1 (NKJV)
To the saints and faithful brethren in Christ who are in Colosse
—Colossians 1:2 (NKJV)

Tragedy [Unhealthy anxiety]

And we know that God causes everything to work together for the good of those who love God and are called according to his purpose for them.
—Romans 8:28 (NLT)
Each one of you will put to flight a thousand of the voice, for the LORD your God fights for you, just as he has promised.
—Joshua 23:10 (NLT)
Though I am surrounded by troubles, you will preserve me against the anger of my enemies. You will clench your fist against my angry enemies! Your power will save me.
—Psalm 138:7 (NLT)
You both precede and follow me. You place your hand of blessing on my head. Such knowledge is too wonderful for me, too great for me to know!
—Psalm 139: 5-6 (NLT)
My child, don't lose sight of good planning and insight. Hang on to them.
—Proverbs 3 (NLT)
But no weapon that can hurt you has ever been forged. Any accuser who takes you to court will be dismissed as a liar. This is what GOD's servants can expect. I'll see to it that everything works out for the best." GOD's Decree.
—Isaiah 54 (MSG)

But I'll deliver you on that doomsday. You won't be handed over to those men whom you have good reason to fear.
—Jeremiah 39 (MSG)

The LORD is my shepherd; I have everything I need. He lets me rest in green meadows; he leads me beside peaceful streams. He renews my strength. He guides me along right paths, bringing honor to his name. Even when I walk through the dark valley of death, I will not be afraid, for you are close beside me. Your rod and your staff protect and comfort me. You prepare a feast for me in the presence of my enemies. You welcome me as a guest, anointing my head with oil. My cup overflows with blessings. Surely your goodness and unfailing love will pursue me all the days of my life, and I will live in the house of the LORD forever.
—Psalm 23 (NIV)

Do not fear people who can kill the body. They cannot kill the spirit. But fear the one who can destroy both spirit and body in hell.
—Matthew 10:28 (WE) Who is going to harm you if you are eager to do good? But even if you should suffer for what is right, you are blessed. Do not fear what they fear; do not be frightened.
—1 Peter 3:13-14 (NIV)

GOD met me more than halfway; he freed me from my anxious fears. —Psalm 34:4 (MSG) Do not be anxious about anything, but in everything, by prayer and petition, with thanksgiving, present your requests to God.
—Philippians 4:6 (NIV)

Twenty Questions for the Voice

1. What's the evidence? Ask yourself, "Would this Voice message hold up in a court of law, or is it circumstantial?" Just because the newspaper is late one day doesn't mean you can't count on anything. Demand a fair trial before you let the Voice convict you.

2. Is the Voice making a mistake in assuming what causes what? Determining causes is rarely simple. Example: Many women think they're fat because they have no willpower. Scientists have been studying obesity for years and they know causes are not simple. They know the reasons are partly biological, social, cultural, psychological, familial and economic. Saying lack of will power causes obesity to be an oversimplification. Specifics are difficult to pinpoint.

3. Is the Voice confusing an opinion with a fact? This can lead to trouble — especially if the Voice calls you names and gets you to believe them as gospel. There is an old story that makes this point: How many legs would a dog have if you called the tail a leg? Five? Wrong! The answer is four. Calling a tail a leg doesn't make it so. Don't let the Voice sway you with opinions — look for the facts.

4. Is the Voice close enough to the situation to really know what's happening? One woman's Voice said, "The bosses upstairs don't like your department's work and want to get rid of all of you." How does the Voice know what they're thinking upstairs? The Voice is not up there with them. You have to rely on what you know as fact. The woman's Voice, as it turned out, was basing this notion on a false rumor.

5. Is the Voice getting you to think in all-or-none terms? Does the Voice get you to see the world in either/or terms ("You're fat and ugly and everyone else is beautiful")? Just about everything is in degrees and on a continuum. Even a person's physical sex (male or female) is not always a clear-cut issue: some people's hormonal makeup is such that it's a toss-up whether they're male or female.

6. Is the Voice using ultimatum words in its messages? ("You should always be nice or no one will like you.") The Voice places unfair ultimatums on you with these words. These words are not merely trivial — they relate directly to how you will eventually feel and act.

7. Is the Voice taking examples out of context? One student let the Voice convince her that she'd been given a bad letter of recommendation. The Voice told her the teacher said in the letter that she was narrow and rigid. When she reread the letter more carefully, she saw the teacher had written, "She has high principles." It was really a positive letter and the Voice had taken this part out of context.

8. Is the Voice being dishonest? Most likely! It tries to fool you by denying the truth, making excuses, and misplacing the blame. One depressed woman, speeding on the freeway, heard her Voice say, "You hope they catch you and put you in jail." When she thought about it for a moment, she realized how stupid this was.

9. Where is the Voice getting its information? Always consider the source from where the Voice gets its information. People have their own reasons for what they say. Is the Voice using unreliable sources or spreaders of gloom to tell you how rotten life is? Why let the Voice use these people to define reality for you?

10. Is the Voice confusing a low probability event (a rare occurrence) with a high probability one? One person, a mailman, caught his Voice saying to him, "Your boss will probably fire you for missing three days of work." But as he reflected on it, he said to the Voice, "When was the last time they fired anyone at the post office?"

11. Is the Voice assuming every situation is the same? Is the Voice conveniently forgetting to take into consideration time, location, and subtle differences between situations? For example, it might say, "Because you dropped out of school twenty years ago, you'll fail this time, too."

12. Is the Voice focusing on irrelevant factors? The Voice will often try to build a case for being depressed by asking a person, "What about Uganda, starving children, and Hitler?" It's highly unfortunate that there's misery and evil in the world, but it's irrelevant to a person who is depressed. By all means, do what you can to alleviate the suffering of others, but letting the Voice get you depressed over it won't help.

13. Is the Voice blinding you to your strengths? When people let the Voice rule their thoughts, they overlook the problems they have solved in the past. I am continually amazed at people's ability to handle adversity once they get rid of the Voice and think for themselves. Ask yourself how you handled situations like these in the past.

14. What do you want when the Voice is gone? What are your personal goals? Who do you want to be? Do you want to get the most out of life? Does believing the Voice when it tells you that life is rotten going to get you what you want? Is the Voice doing you any good?

15. How would you look at things if the Voice were not controlling your thinking? Does it make sense to believe a cold sore is the worst thing that could happen to you? How would others (neutral observers) interpret the same situation? Imagine how you'll react to something once you have defeated the Voice.

16. What can you do to solve the problem? Is the Voice helping to problem solve (generate solutions)? If your kids are fighting and the plumbing is stopped up, letting the Voice get you to concentrate on the "unfairness of it all" doesn't lead to solutions.

17. Is the Voice asking questions that have no answers? "How can you redo the past?"..."How can you make someone act differently?" "How can a relationship that's ended not be over?" Questions like these can sometimes be answered with other questions. "Why should this happen to you?" Answer: "Why shouldn't it?" "What if something terrible happens?" Answer: "What can I do about it?" Letting the Voice emphasize unanswerable questions is another way of letting the Voice convince you the world might be different than it really is.

18. Is the Voice using Keywords that you might be missing? Maybe you are fighting the Voice over the Keyword "worthless" for the thousandth time, but this time you are not making any headway. It might be that "should" — or some other Keyword — is buried somewhere in that pile of mental garbage.

19. What are the advantages and disadvantages of buying into the Voice? What are the advantages of letting the Voice say "You hate this house, you hate this neighborhood, and you hate this city and everything in it." There are probably very few. One major disadvantage in letting the Voice dominate your thinking is that it will stop you from getting your share of life's pleasures.

20. What difference will this make in a week, a year or ten years? Will anyone remember in ten years (let alone care) that you made a stupid remark at a party or had dandruff on your sweater? The Voice gets people to believe that their mistakes will be frozen forever in others' minds.

Typical Voice Fighting Errors

1. Mislabeling your emotion. You must be certain whether you are dealing with a constructive or destructive emotion. If you are fighting the Voice merely because you feel emotional pain, you might be wasting your time if the pain is the result of a constructive emotion. This error is very common to the beginning Voice fighter. You can tell when this is happening by comparing your results to your effort. If you are spending considerable time and energy in fighting the Voice but making no gains, the chances are that you are really dealing with a constructive emotion.

2. Stopping interrogation prematurely. When you first begin Voice Fighting, you may find it difficult to continue saying "So what if..." to the Voice. Often, after several attempts at this, the Voice throws something heavy-duty at you and you buckle under by trying to answer back or worse yet agreeing with what it is saying. By writing down what you are saying, you will find it easier to go back over the fight and see if you are giving in too soon. Remember that you can say "So what if..." for hours, days, or weeks if you have to.

3. Getting confused when you win. Many times a first time Voice Fighter will do much better than expected. If the Voice shuts up after a few volleys, you can be in for quite a shock. Many people get flustered at this point because it is such a new experience. Some individuals even become upset because they don't know what to do next. What you do next is enjoy yourself. Take advantage of the Voice's absence to have some fun.

4. Moving too quickly against the Voice. At this point in your Voice Fighting, you need to perfect your defensive tactics. Later on, you will learn to take the offensive against the Voice. To play good defense, you must know your opponent and wait for him to commit himself. Let the Voice lead, and then, when you see what is happening, pounce!

5. Shortcutting your Basic Voice Fighting Response. Impatience can get you into a real jam. The Voice will tell you not to waste your time going through all five steps. As usual, it is lying to you. If you use just the arguments, you will diminish the impact of your Voice Fighting. Always use your Voice Fighting Kit, even if you are sure you have it memorized. Be sure to follow the flow chart exactly as you have it. Later, when you have become an expert, you can take shortcuts and do quite well against the Voice.

6. Insisting on reasons. You will defeat your entire purpose if you insist on finding the reasons for your problems. The reasons are unimportant at this time in your life. They merely satisfy your curiosity. Finding reasons can be done after you have become victorious over the Voice.

7. Memorizing the Voice Fighting Kit. After you've been using your Kit for several months, the Voice will try to shame you into leaving it behind by telling you that you shouldn't have to rely on a pack of stupid index cards anymore. Of course if you buy this suggestion, the Voice has a better shot at you when you are stressed and confused.

8. Mental Voice Fighting. Although this is the style of fighting you eventually want to become proficient at, the present is too soon to rely on this style to give you much help. The Voice is still too fast for you. You must slow it down, which is done using the other two fighting methods: verbal and written.

9. Relying on Distraction. When you begin to have some victories against the Voice, you begin to have more and more good days. It is very tempting on your good days to completely forget everything that you have learned about the Voice. Your Good-Day Rule of thumb is: on good days you work twice as hard! Remember to schedule in Voice Fighting times every day. If, at the appointed time, the Voice is nowhere to be seen, then use rehearsal fighting or replay fighting. The rehearsal method is like any athletic practice session. It is to prepare you for the actual contest. You think of something happening in the immediate future that the Voice will use against you. Try to anticipate the keywords and practice fighting them in advance. The replay

method is like watching a videotape after the big game. It is a means of finding your weaknesses and strengthening them in preparation for the rematch. Practicing past fights can be an excellent means of improving your self-confidence and Voice Fighting ability.

10. Hearing only one keyword. If you have a persistent Voice, it is possible that one particular keyword may overshadow all the others. For example, your Voice may continually use tragedy or should to the exclusion of the other keywords. This actually gives you an advantage, because it is easy for you to discover the keyword and fight back. If this happens to you, you only have to watch out for the emergence of the other keywords as you gain more power over the main one.

Discussion Questions

1. How long do you think you have had the Voice in your life? Describe some of the damage it has done to you.

2. Talk about the fact that you will never get rid of the Voice. Your goal is to totally dominate it so it won't make any difference of it hangs around forever.

3. What might be any advantages for practicing Voice Fighting with someone else? You may use someone in your study group or your Grace Partner. Can you think of anyone else who might be helpful in this regard?

4. What are your options if you find that Voice Fighting is not working very well?

5. Have someone in your group play the "victim" as the rest of the group plays the "Voice." Have the victim stop when they identify a keyword and use the voice fighting steps to zap it with one or more of the truth statements.

For more information on Voice Fighting see chapter 7 in *The Worry Free Life*

The Worry Free Life
Session #8: Christian Affirmations

You welcomed me as if I were an angel of God, as Christ Jesus himself. What, then, happened to your positive attitude?
— Galatians 4:14-15 (ISV)

Bringing Back the Flowers

Now that you have the tools to chase the Voice out of your garden, it's time to rebuild the landscape. Rebuilding your garden landscape produces new self-confidence and increases your personal power. Since the Voice has taken so much of your mental capacity, you may have empty spaces to fill as you continue to move it out of your life. Using Christian Affirmations will help you to backfill the emptiness left behind as the Voice continues its retreat. The more you can fill, the harder it will be for the Voice to attempt a comeback.

Christian Affirmations

An affirmation is a form of reprogramming your mental state with the beliefs and perceptions that are best for you. Begin by creating a Christian Affirmation bank. Develop a savings account of strong sayings about yourself.

Resources for finding affirmations

a. Bible
b. Sermons
c. Inspirational books
d. Web sites

Sample websites:
  http://www.affirmations.com/
  http://www.positiveaffirmations.com/
  http://www.vitalaffirmations.com/

List some other sources you can use to come up with Christian affirmations that could work for your life.

The best method for finding affirmations with a punch is to steal them from the Voice. By changing what it is saying into the positive opposite you can use its strength against itself. Here are some examples. The first line (italicized) is a typical Voice comment. The next line is a possible Christian affirmation that you might use.

You Suck. I have infinite worth and unlimited potential.

Nobody likes you.
People love and adore me if they know me.

If anything can go wrong it probably will.
Whatever happens, I can handle it and learn from it.

You hate your children's friends.
Their friends are their choices. My children learn from their mistakes.

Your boss is a jerk.
My boss's mood swings are his responsibility.

You'll never find someone to love you.
I'll always be able to attract a worthwhile mate.

You are so worried about money.
God has blessed me with more riches than I need.

Your getting so old, fat and wrinkled.
I am not my body. I am God's complete, perfect, and worthy child just the way I am.

You're overwhelmed!
I can work hard at being peaceful and not let anyone bring me down.

You can't take this!
Infinite patience produces immediate results.

God hates you.
God is creative, kind and loving; never condemning.

You'll never get it all done.
I will get done what I need to get done.

Your Wildest Dreams

These Christian Affirmations must be specific and unbelievable (see chapter 8 in The Worry Free Life). Another clue for finding a good Christian Affirmation is let your imagination run wild by thinking of the most exciting things happening in your life that you have never thought possible. For example:

- ⚜ "I can be loved by people who I used to think were better than me."
- ⚜ "I can have a rich, fulfilling and exciting life."
- ⚜ "I can be financially secure for the rest of my life."
- ⚜ "I can have a worry free life."
- ⚜ "I can cope with the most difficult family members in my life."
- ⚜ "I can choose who I want in my life."

My 5 Wildest Dreams

_____

_____

_____

_____

_____

Develop A Christian Affirmation Bank

Now that you have some ideas on where to find Christian Affirmations, you need to begin your own list. We call this list your Christian Affirmation Bank. Over the course of time you will make deposits and withdrawals from your bank. Use the form below to begin this process.

Potential Christian Affirmation	Possible situations where this might be helpful

How to Use Christian Affirmations

You can practice affirmations three different ways:

1. Mentally
2. Out loud
3. On Paper

Written Examples:

Christian Affirmation	Voice	Me
I am a winner.	You? What a laugh!	Just wait to see who has the last laugh.
I can take complete charge of my life.	I've been with you forever. You'll never get rid of me.	Guess what. You're due for a permanent vacation.
I'm going to enjoy having fun with my friends again.	Your friends don't even remember you—and don't want to.	I'm going to tell them about you and when they see you lurking about they're going to gang up on you.

Practice Christian Affirmations daily. Use a different Christian Affirmation each day. This skill is not to be used *instead* of Voice Fighting but along side it. Our rule of thumb is: *On bad days fight the Voice; on good days use Christian Affirmations.*

For more information on Christian Affirmations, see chapter 8 in The Worry Free Life

Discussion Questions

1. Read Jeremiah 29:11. Since God only wants the best for you, what would that look like for you?

2. What are some Voice lies that are holding you back from achieving your dreams?

3. What are your best qualities? How has the Voice kept you from accepting and practicing them?

4. If God were to brag about you, what would He say to others about you?

For more information on the material in this lesson, see Chapter 8 in *The Worry Free Life*

The Worry Free Life
Session #9: Replanting Your Garden

. . . if you plant in the soil of your spiritual nature, you will harvest everlasting life .
— *Galatians 6:8 (GW)*

Christian Rights

Take the matter of our right to have rights. We Christians sometimes act as if other people have rights but we do not. For example, we sometimes believe that we do not have the right to protest unfair treatment or criticism because it would violate Christ's standard of turning the other cheek. Sometimes we feel guilty when we feel too happy or when life is going too well for us. Perhaps the least appreciated right among Christians is the right to make mistakes. We find it all too easy to feel guilty when we mess up.

The grace-filled perspective is to recognize that God wants us to live an abundant life, and that includes basing our life on God-given human rights. God wants us to access our humanity at the deepest level possible.

Garden Tool #1: Christian Selfishness?

We've all been told that's it is unchristian to be selfish. We've not been told that there are two kinds of selfishness. Definitions of selfishness:

· *Unchristian*: "Taking care of your needs without ever helping others take care of their needs."
· *Christian*: "Taking care of your needs first and then helping others get their needs met."

Some Christians believe that the opposite of being selfish is to be a doormat. You can't give other people water if your well is dry. As a human being, you have certain rights that you were given at birth. In what areas of your life do you need to be more selfish (Christian) in order to serve God better?

Read through your list of Christian rights in chapter 9 of *The Worry Free Life*. Identify those that are difficult for you. Rewrite these in the space below.

Read this list aloud every morning soon after awakening. Many people find it helpful to tape this list to the bathroom mirror.

65

Garden Tool #2: Personal Responsibility

Personal responsibility means accepting the consequences of your actions without blame or excuse. Some people do not want to accept the consequences of their bad decisions—only their good decisions. Admitting wrongdoing is not a common behavior in our society. By acting non-responsibly, you allow yourself to become a victim. God's grace is intended to free us from these societal bonds and become victorious.

The Victim	The Victor
...sees few or no choices available.	...sees life full of choices.
..sees problems as hopeless barriers.	...sees problems as challenges to be solved.
...believes people who get ahead are just lucky	...believes that people who get ahead do so primarily out of their own efforts and preparation.
...is resistant to change and unwilling to seriously consider other options.	...is open to change and willing to change for a good reason.
...believes destiny is determined by external circumstances beyond control.	...believes destiny is determined by personal efforts.
...feels unable to influence future.	...feels empowered to influence future.
...is uninvolved in personal development.	...is totally involved in personal development.
...gives little consideration to personal desires in relationships.	...gives serious consideration to personal desires in relationships.
...allows others and outside events to make personal decisions.	...actively makes personal decisions.
...has either no personal objectives or sets unrealistic goals.	...sets realistic and achievable personal objectives.
...avoids future life planning.	...carefully plans personal future.

— Which column best represents you?

— How can you use all the skills you have learned this far to help you live as a Victor?

Garden Tool #3: Social Responsibility

Social responsibility is one of the most important elements of the Big "H." People whose lives are inclusive of the needs of others have a better quality of life than those whose goals do not include the well-being of others. Jesus' entire life was devoted to the higher purpose of caring for others. He cared for those whom society had marginalized. He shunned the popular people, the people with power, wealth, and fame.

He taught us that this is the surest way to be in a right relationship with God. Some of you may have trouble accepting responsibility for yourself but have no qualms being responsible for the rest of the world. In our society, women have been taught they must take care of everyone around them. Since everyone has problems, you can find yourself loaded down with the problems of other people.

When you find yourself taking on the unnecessary problems of other people, we call that activity Monkey Collecting. This comes from the phrase, "A monkey on your back." Everyone has monkeys on their back—some more than others. The world has two kinds of people: Monkey Givers and Monkey Collectors. Many Christians are monkey collectors. You may deliberately invite others to give their problems to you. Maybe you want to fix the problems of everyone around you. Or maybe you just want to "be there" for others with problems.

The most common monkeys that people collect are the feelings of other people. You cannot hurt another person's feelings because feelings come from thoughts. Since you cannot control another person's thoughts , you cannot hurt their feelings. Only the other person's thoughts can generate the feelings they are experiencing. You want to avoid taking responsibility for another person's feelings while taking full responsibility for your behavior toward that person. You are responsible for what you do to another person—not how people feel about what you do.

— Whose monkeys do you take?

— Who actively gives you their monkeys?

Garden Tool #4: Risk Taking

If you desire the life that God wants for you, you need to take risks. We are more alive when we take healthy risks. Reasons for taking healthy risks:

(1) All life is more intense: love, joy, faith, hope.
(2) Relationships with people are deeper and more intimate.
(3) You grow as a human being at a faster rate: spiritually, emotionally, intellectually.
(4) You become more mature.
(5) Others respect you more

Some problems are so familiar that people are afraid to take the risk of giving them up. When you risk, you become vulnerable. We don't take risks because we want a guaranteed outcome. Humans are not very good at risk assessment. Since risk can be difficult, some people use their problems as protective cocoons against the real world.

Choosing to risk strengthens your self image. It shows that you have confidence in your judgment and are willing to overcome fear, boredom, or complacency in order to bring about change. Deliberately taking a chance implies that your decision to pursue a certain source is rational. By risking — whether it's getting married or divorced, moving to a new community or career — you show yourself that you are prepared to deal with either failure or success.

If you succeed, you will enjoy a new vitality and sense of accomplishment. If you don't, the experience will strengthen your resolve to risk again because you've tested your courage and know you're able to go on.

— What have been some of the cocoons in your life that you have used to protect you from getting hurt by taking risks?

Forgiveness

The next step to complete your journey in grace is to learn to forgive those who have hurt you. Lewis Smedes, late professor of theology and ethics at Fuller Seminary was a leader in the field of forgiveness. He emphasized that forgiving someone was not for their benefit but for ours. He explained this by saying, "When we forgive, we set a prisoner free and discover that the prisoner we set free is us." Forgiveness is necessary for strong transgressions — violations that leave lasting wounds and hurts. Often there is no reason to have a connection to this person. The transgression may be so severe that it would be foolhardy to have a relationship with this person. Nevertheless, we need to forgive the abuser, no matter how intolerable that may appear. The purpose of forgiveness is to rewrite your history and cancel the debt. When a person has abused us we tend to want at least 4 things to happen:

— *Apology*. Why have you wanted the abuser to understand how badly he or she hurt you?

— *Penance*. In what way have you wanted the abuser to feel sorry and remorseful?

68

— Compensation. How have you wanted the transgressor to pay for the transgression?

— Retribution. Have you wanted him or her to be hurt as badly as you were? Why?

The four steps for forgiving someone are:

1. Self discovery
2. Considering forgiveness
3. Learning forgiveness skills
4. Deepening forgiveness

Step One: Self Discovery

— What exactly happened to you?

— When did this happen?

— How often did it happen?

— Who was unfair?

— Why do you think the person was unfair?

Step Two – Consider Forgiveness

Your first step is to finally consider that forgiveness of the abuser might be a realistic option. To help you in this consideration, you need to carefully understand what forgiveness is. Forgiveness is the combination of abandoning resentment (which is a natural response) while adopting friendlier attitudes towards the abuser (which is an unnatural response). You may need time before you can reach that place in your life where you balance both of these pieces within your being. You need to be willing to accept the difficulty of this requirement.

— Write in the space below how you might go about considering the possibility of forgiving the person who caused you so much hurt.

Step Three – Learning the Skills of Forgiveness [4 parts]

The first part is called **reinterpretation**. This is a process in which you reconsider the entire painful event within a new and fresh perspective. This exercise is one the Voice will work hard to keep from happening.

— How can you begin to see the abuser as a human being rather than as evil incarnate.

The second part of this step is called **empathy and compassion**. Many people find that experiencing empathy for the offender needs to begin in microscopic doses.

— What are some small steps you could take (when you are ready) to begin to experience empathy for the offender?

The third part in this step is referred to as **acceptance**. The part requires you to bear the pain. This is unnatural and can often be intensely painful, which is why people are able to forgive and remain victimized. It is a transitional part that involves letting go of fighting the pain and hurt. As with all healthy emotional pain, complete acceptance of the emotion will cause it to pass.

— What skills have you learned so far from the book and Study Guide that can help you accept the pain of forgiving your abuser?

The fourth part in this step is to **give a moral gift**. Forgiveness, to be complete, must be expressed. If the offender is not available or appropriate for contact, this will not apply to you.

— If appropriate, how would express your forgiveness to your abuser?

Step Four – Deepening the Forgiveness

Many people who suffer from events not of their making have a need to find meaning in their suffering. Meaning can be found in many different places. Some people find it in the Bible (book of Job, the concept of the Suffering Servant, etc.). Others see how it changed their lives for the better ("Now that I can look back on it, I realize I am a better and stronger person for it having happened.").

— How can you interpret your pain and suffering to make it meaningful?

Discussion Questions

1. As you read through the list of rights in The Worry Free Life, what makes you uncomfortable about the concept of Christian rights?

2. In Matthew 14:13, Jesus exercised His Christian right to be alone and to heal. In what circumstances could you emulate him and also exercise your right to heal?

3. Read the beatitude in Matthew 5:6. How can your taking more personal responsibility be seen as righteousness?

4. In the space below, show how you have benefitted from risks you have taken.

For more information, see chapter 9 in *The Worry Free Life*.

The Worry Free Life
Session #10: The Behavior Domino

"Like the Holy One who called you, be holy yourselves also in all your behavior."
— 1 Peter 1:15, NASB

Difficulties with the Behavior Domino

Many people believe that once you have made significant changes to your internal self—have become a new person—that you will start acting differently. But all one needs to do is to look around with open eyes to know such an assumption calls for caution.

Target Behaviors

Selecting a Goal
The first step is to decide to prioritize what you need to change. What behavior or habit do you want to change first? In making your decision, it will help to identify two categories of behaviors. One set of behaviors is composed of positive actions that are not being done, and the other set is made up of negative actions that are being done.

Think of a bad habit or other recurring behavior that you want to change. Is it a behavior you want to do more often or less often?

Replacement Behaviors
Replacement behaviors are based on the notion that all destructive behaviors have incompatible, opposite behaviors that can be used for your target or goal behaviors.

For each of the excessive behaviors (ones you do too often) identify an opposite behavior that you can make happen more often.

Making Observations
You will begin your observations by tracking and recording the frequency of both your destructive behaviors and your replacement behaviors (how often each behavior occurs). Keep this behavior log for a about a week—long enough to get a sense that your observations are representative.

After keeping your log for a few days, what have you discovered about the behavior you want to change?

Using Motivators

When scientists discovered that what followed our actions was more of a cause than what preceded our actions, it did not seem to make sense. After decades of research and innumerable hours of clinical experience, we now know, beyond any doubt, that consequences control our behavior. These consequences can be external (extrinsic) or internal (intrinsic). You will learn to manage your behavior by effectively managing the consequences of your behavior. Remember, there are two types of consequences: reinforcers (rewards), and reducers (punishment). Reinforcers are consequences that increase behavior; reducers are consequences that decrease behaviors. Research has proven that reinforcers are more effective and predictable than reducers. Since we want you to work on increasing behaviors (target behaviors for your deficit behaviors and replacement behaviors for your excessive behaviors) you will concentrate on using reinforcers.

What could you use as a reward for increasing your desired behavior? Here are some categories you might consider:
- ☐ Social rewards (spending time with people you like)
- ☐ Activity rewards (for a lengthy list of examples see www.TheWorryFreeLife.com/funthingstodo
- ☐ Material rewards (Giving yourself something you really want)

The Voice's Tricks

As you can imagine, the Voice won't be happy with your using the skills in this chapter. It would be more than content if you just worked on improving your emotional state and your thoughts without ever translating them into action. Many psychologists are familiar with people telling them how much some experience has changed their lives because they feel so much better. Upon closer examination, their behavior has not changed. This step—the behavior domino—is sometimes the lengthiest step in the entire change process. The length depends on how many behaviors you want to change and how deeply ingrained they are. Since you have come this far in your progress, forgetting the Voice is easy. But it will always be there and will always try to win back control.

Discussion Questions

1. Read Romans 7:19. Even Paul struggled with behavior change. What habits in your life have been plaguing you for years and years?

2. Some people think rewards are bribes. Discuss the differences (see chapter 10 in The Worry Free Life)

3. How could you use other people in your life to help you implement your new behavior change skills?

4. Most people tell you to work on your behavior first ("Just stop drinking!; "Don't be so angry"). Why do we ask you to work on your behavior as the last step? (*Hint*: See the Dominoes)

The Worry Free Life
Session #11: Accepting God's Grace

Grace to you and peace from God our Father and the Lord Jesus Christ.
— *Romans 1:7 (ASV)*

Rebuilding the Positive

As a psychologist, Terry discovered long ago that when people release themselves from their emotional pain, they do not automatically experience the Big "H". Earlier in this book, we introduced you to Martin Seligman, psychologist and past president of the American Psychological Association, who began a new movement in mental health. This research-based movement, called Positive Psychology, concentrates on what makes people thrive and experience fulfillment. Just as Christ transcended the ordinary and mundane aspects of life, we, too, can focus on the brighter side of life: looking forward instead of backward, reaching beyond ourselves, and accepting personal progress as a "receding horizon."

Quality of Life

A better quality of life can result in living longer, it can increase your problem-solving ability for life's annoyances and even contribute to helping people find and keep better jobs. Most importantly, people who have a solid quality of life find their social lives are stronger and more satisfying. People who are more satisfied with life will likely be more energetic, forgiving, and generous than others who are less satisfied with their lives. Increasing your quality of life can even make you less susceptible to disease. Obtaining a good quality of life is where you want your life to go after you have minimized the influence of the Voice in your life. For some people, getting rid of the Voice does not automatically improve quality of life.

Psychological Wellbeing: The Six Ingredients

Wellbeing is the ultimate goal you want to reach. It means a life that is in harmony with God, the world, and yourself. As the Voice and all the problems it brings begins to recede from your life, you can spend more time on making your personal strengths stronger. You can now spend more time working on personal experiences that increase your wellbeing. These are the six areas that you will want to emphasize:

Increase Autonomy.
As Paul taught us, being a Christian is not about living under a specific set of rules. We increase our personal independence by being free and living in God's grace and love.

Strengthen Environmental Mastery.
Christians refuse to live in a toxic environment because it eats away at our soul. Although we can grow and learn from difficult situations, there are some we need to avoid if possible.

Encourage Personal Growth.
The Worry Free Life is all about personal growth. We have taken you to the next step showing you how to do what is good for you. You are already well on your way because you have been reading and studying The Worry Free Life.

Develop Positive Relations with Others.
God has made us to live in community. The more we can experience healthy and intimate relationships, the more we are able to be one with God.

Identify Purpose in Life.
Purpose is always identified individually. You must use all your new skills to find your true self. Seek out as many sources as possible to find your gifts. Here is where you will find your purpose in life.

Foster Self-acceptance.
Love is the driving force of the universe. God is love. Until you love yourself fully, you will also feel an emptiness in your heart.

Use the weekly worksheet below to increase your psychological wellbeing. Each day write in the squares anything you have done to work on any of the six wellbeing components. How many you work on is up to you. Go at your own pace, but try to keep it steady and positive.

	Increase Autonomy	Environmental Mastery	Personal Growth	Positive Relations	Purpose in Life	Self Acceptance
Sunday						
Monday						
Tuesday						
Wednesday						
Thursday						
Friday						
Saturday						

Hope

Hope is also one of the great themes of Christianity (1 Corinthians 13:13). In the history of the Christian church, it has been a major adaptive response to times of stress and desperation. Christians have found hope to be a necessary ingredient for emotional survival during times of disastrous circumstances such as severe loss or incurable and terminal illnesses. Some scholars make a distinction between wishing and hoping. They believe that wishing is more concrete and directed toward specific outcomes (a suitable mate, gaining a special reward). Hope is more global, such as hoping to be set free, to be understood and recognized, or to be reconciled to other people.

Sometimes people see hope as a passive waiting for something good to happen. From his research, Dr. Snyder shows that hope is more than wishful thinking. It involves a willfulness and resoluteness along with a direction for getting to a goal. The writer to the Hebrews talked about such an attitude, too. "We who have run for our very lives to God have every reason to grab the promised hope with both hands and never let go" (Hebrews 6:18, MSG).

There are two parts to hope: knowing where you would like to be in your life and knowing there is a path to get there.

What do you hope your life to be like in five years?

What are some of the paths you can explore to get you there?

Gratitude

Using Gratitude to Enhance the past

One way of overcoming your memories of the past is to learn to experience more gratitude for the good things in your past. Gratitude increases your ability to savor and appreciate the good events that have happened. It works to increase your life satisfaction because it amplifies good memories about your past in three ways. Gratitude intensifies good memories. Gratitude makes the memories more frequent. Gratitude connects your memories to a more positive outlook.

Once you have dealt with forgiving those who have brought you pain in the past, you can focus on the good things in your past. In the following table, identify at least one positive event that happened to you in each of the developmental life stages.

Early childhood	
Pre-teens	
Adolescence	
Young adult	
Adult	

Using Gratitude to Enhance The Present

Blessings have a long heritage in the history of Christianity. To keep you within this tradition, we want you to begin some exercises to increase your gratitude in the present time. The first is called the Self Appreciation Exercise. The second is the Gratitude Visit.

Self Appreciation Exercise

This is a daily exercise best done in the evening. Start by identifying at least three success that day. These events do not have to be of monumental significance. Like the Success Journal, the small things can often be the most important things for you to dwell upon. They might not have been pleasant or easy. For example, you may have found yourself in a confrontation where you stood your ground.

1. Focus on the skills you used to make these events good for you.

2. How have these events influenced your life, and possibly others because you have achieved these victories?

3. Add these victories right into your Success Journal each evening. Fall asleep thinking about what you have written.

4. Recent research has shown that after two weeks of doing this (and similar exercises) you will experience a significant increase in the level of happiness (Big "H") in your life.

The Gratitude Visit

This exercise has been shown to have a powerful impact in the lives of those who use it. It is being used by permission of psychologist Dr. Seligman (Seligman, M. E. P. (2004). *Authentic happiness: Using the new positive psychology to realize your potential for lasting fulfillment*. New York: Free Press.)

Select one important person from your past who has made a major positive difference in your life and to whom you have never fully expressed your thanks.

▶ Do not confound this selection with newfound romantic love or with the possibility of future gain

▶ Write a testimonial just long enough to cover one laminated page.

▶ Take your time composing this. This may take several weeks, e.g., composing on a bus, as you fall asleep at night.

▶ Invite that person to your home or travel to that person's home.

▶ It is important you do this face to face, not just in writing or on the phone.

▶ Do not tell the person the purpose of the visit in advance; a simple "I just want to see you" will suffice.

▶ Wine and cheese do not matter, but bring a laminated version of your testimonial with you as a gift.

▶ When all settles down, read your testimonial aloud slowly, with expression, and with eye contact.

▶ Let the other person react unhurriedly.

▶ Reminisce together about the concrete events that make this person so important to you.

Discussion Questions

1. Proverbs 28:19 tells us that merely wishing for a better life does not work. Working, instead of wishing, is the key. By working to develop hope, wellbeing, gratitude and other skills you will produce the growth you want in your life. Discuss times in your life when you had the most growth and identify how much effort you were putting into it.

2. Read Proverbs 23.18. This verse tells us there is always hope. Since your attitudes and actions are the source of hope, how can you tap into this during difficult times?

3. Make a list of at least 25 things you can be grateful for now. Share this with your small group, a friend or anyone of your choosing. Put the list in a prominent place (refrigerator?) and look at it daily. Add to it as more things come to mind.

4. Read Proverbs 23:9 and discuss how this applies to the topic of environmental mastery.

The Worry Free Life
Session #12: Final Review

"Test everything. Hold on to the good."
— 1 Thessalonians 5:21 (NIV)

Quiz (answers following)

1. Two significant reasons for continued writing:

2. Describe "silent assumptions" or "automatic thinking."

3. Changing the pronouns from "I" to "you" in your writing is helpful because:

4. The Voice's purpose in our lives is to:
   a.   Destroy us
   b.   Trick us into self-destructive thoughts, emotions and behaviors
   c.   Keep us from growing spiritually
   d.   All the above

5. Other people's feelings are: (choose all that are correct)
   a.   Your responsibility
   b.   None of your business
   c.   Outside your property lines
   d.   Usually stupid and silly

6. TRUE or FALSE: The Voice makes people feel guilty when they make a mistake.

7. TRUE or FALSE: The emotion of helplessness makes us escape or run away.

8. What is a keyword?

9. Give some examples of keywords that can generate depression.

10. The four things we can control and are responsible for in our Garden are:

11. Even when someone violates your rights they still have

12. Write out one new affirmation you will incorporate into your life from now on:

13. "God Reigns In His Delightful Universe" is a mnemonic that helps us remember the Voice's six cancerous emotions which are:

14. In what way is anxiety different from fear?

15. Emotions are like grapes because they

16. The pest that tries to convince us that we should not waste time and always be very productive is called the _____ pest.

17. The pest that tries to convince us that we know what others are thinking is called the _____ pest.

18. TRUE or FALSE: There is only one correct way to interpret any given situation.

19. Increasing your gratitude is important because:

20. Why is forgiving others important?

21. Which of the following steps is not involved in the forgiveness of another person?

       a. Considering the decision to forgive
       b. Establishing a healthy relationship with the abuser
       c. Self discovery
       d. Deepening the forgiveness
       e. Learning the skills of forgiveness

22. TRUE or FALSE: Once the Voice is cleared out of your life, your behavior will automatically become more pure.

23. Which of the following are not a God-given right?

       a.   The right to refuse a request
       b.   The right to waste time
       c.   The right to always put others first
       d.   The right to protect your privacy
       e.   The right to control your unruly children
       f.   The right to be selfish

24.   TRUE or FALSE: I can't change the way I am because of what happened to me in the past.

Answers to Final Quiz

1. Two significant reasons for continued writing:

      a. 95% of all our thoughts are non-conscious
      b. Writing is the only way to minimize the effect of the Voice's two favorite weapons: speed and secrecy

2. Describe "silent assumptions" or "automatic thinking."
      a.   Thoughts that are not audible
      b.   Thoughts that occur so rapidly and quietly we cannot perceive them
      c.   Thoughts that have a profound ability to make us feel lousy or great

3. Changing the pronouns from "I" to "you" in your writing is helpful because: it helps to remind you that these destructive thoughts come from outside of you. These thoughts do not belong to you but come from the Voice.

4. The Voice's purpose in our lives is to: (d) All the above

5. Other people's feelings are (choose all that are correct): c. Outside your property lines

6. The Voice makes people feel guilty when they make a mistake: True

7. The emotion of helplessness makes us escape or run away: True

8. What is a keyword? A keyword is a word we discover in our writing that reveals the voice is at work, polluting our thoughts with toxic thinking and self-destructive emotions.

9. Give some examples of keywords that can generate depression: Worthless, deficient, no good, you suck, loser, useless, bad, despicable, good-for-nothing, miserable, hopeless, pathetic, pitiful.

10. The four things we can control and are responsible for in our Garden are:
      a.   Behavior
      b.   Emotions
      c.   Sensations/Stress
      d.   Thoughts

11. Even when someone who violates your rights they still have infinite worth.

12. Write out one new affirmation you will incorporate into your life from now on.

13. "God Reigns In His Delightful Universe" is a mnemonic that helps us remember the Voice's six cancerous emotions which are: a.   Guilt b.   Resentment   c.   Irrational Fear
d.   Helplessness e.   Depression f.   Unhealthy Anxiety

14. In what way is anxiety different from fear? Anxiety is always about the "future" event; Fear is always about the present.

15. Emotions are like grapes because they often come in clusters.

16. The pest that tries to convince us that we should not waste time and be always very productive is called the busy-busy pest.

17. The pest that tries to convince us that we know what others are thinking is called the mind reading pest.

18. There is only one correct way to interpret any given situation. False

19. Increasing your gratitude is important because it helps build healthier relationships and makes you a happier person.

20. Why is forgiving others important? "When we forgive, we set a prisoner free and discover that the prisoner we set free is us."

21. Which of the following steps is not involved in the forgiveness of another person?   b. Establishing a healthy relationship with the abuser

22. Once the Voice is cleared out of your life, your behavior will automatically become more pure. False

23. Which of the following are not a God-given right?
     c.   The right to always put others first
     e.   The right to control your unruly children

24. I can't change the way I am because of what happened to me in the past. False

More on The Worry Free Life

Congratulations! You are well on your way to living the worry free life God intended for you.

Your mind's "Garden" can be free of unhealthy, worrisome thoughts. You just need to prune it regularly.

Authors Dr. Terry Sandbek and Patrick W. Philbrick provide further tools to attack the "weeds" that try to grow back while nurturing the positive growth that has already begun.

1. Visit www.TheWorryFreeLife.com

2. Subscribe to The Worry Free Life monthly newsletter by emailing us at: Subscribe@ TheWorryFreeLife.com

3. Request class materials to start your own small group or life skill class at: www. TheWorryFreeLife.com

4. Receive updates on the latest related publications: books, CDs, sermon ideas, and more by emailing us at: Inquiry@TheWorryFreeLife.com

5. Or, contact the publisher with requests, comments, questions or further information:

Green Valley Publishing LLC
4300 Auburn Bl, Ste 206
Sacramento, California 95841
U.S.A.
(530) 621-3098

You really can live a life free from worry!